Song and
Silence

Song and Silence

ETHNIC REVIVAL ON
CHINA'S SOUTHWEST BORDERS

Sara L. M. Davis

COLUMBIA UNIVERSITY PRESS
NEW YORK

COLUMBIA UNIVERSITY PRESS

Publishers Since 1893

New York   Chichester, West Sussex

Copyright © 2005 Columbia University Press

All rights reserved

Library of Congress Cataloging-in-Publication Data

Davis, Sara L. M. (Sara Leila Margaret), 1967–

Song and silence. Ethnic revival on China's southwest border /

Sara L. M. Davis

p. cm.

Includes bibliographical references and index.

ISBN 0–231–13526–2 (cloth : alk. paper) —

ISBN 0–231–13527–0 (pbk. : alk. paper)

1. Tai (Southeast Asian people) — China — Xishuangbanna
Daizu Zizhiqu. 2. Xishuangbanna Daizu Zizhizhou
(China) — Ethnic relations. I. Title: Ethnic revival on
China's southwest border. II. Title.

DS797.86.X57D38   2005

305.895'9105135 — dc22

2005041292

Columbia University Press books are printed
on permanent and durable acid-free paper.

Printed in the United States of America

Designed by Lisa Hamm

c 10 9 8 7 6 5 4 3 2 1
p 10 9 8 7 6 5 4 3 2 1

Contents

Maps and Illustrations

UNLESS OTHERWISE NOTED, PHOTOS ARE COURTESY OF THE AUTHOR.

Maps

Photos

Acknowledgments

I am grateful to friends and colleagues of many ethnicities in Yunnan, northern Thailand, and Shan State who shared their hospitality and insights during this research but who have asked to remain anonymous. *Feichang ganxie, khawpkhun maak,* and *yindee.*

Several foundations and centers supported this work: ACLS/ Committee for Scholarly Communication with China, American Association of University Women, Yale University's Council on East Asian Studies, and UCLA's Center for Southeast Asian Studies. Special thanks are due to administrative staff in all these places and especially to Peggy Guinan at University of Pennsylvania.

Pat Giersch and Erik Mueggler shared thoughtful suggestions that shaped later stages of the manuscript. Mark Selden acted as my writing coach and foster editor via e-mail for several years. I am also grateful to the following people for enlightening conversations, careful readings, or both: Ai Feng, Susan Blum, Tom Borchert, Gardner Bovingdon, Chayan Vaddhanaphuti, Paul Cohen, Deborah Davis, David Feingold, Valerie Hansen, Sandra Hyde, Charles Keyes, Josef Margraf, Susan McCarthy, Margaret Mills, Andrew Nathan, Heather Peters, Helen Rees, Peggy Swaine, Donald Swearer, Steve Thompson, Wasan Panyagaew, Yang Hui, and Eileen Walsh. I benefited from conversations with many people at Human Rights Watch in New York, at Images Asia/Ecology Desk in Chiang Mai, and at

Lulu's Cafe in New Haven, Conn. I also learned from participants in many AAS and AAA conference panels on Yunnan over the years. Only I am to blame for any errors or faulty conclusions.

I owe significant intellectual debts to two mentors: Victor H. Mair at University of Pennsylvania and Margaret A. Mills at Ohio State University. Both have been inspiring and supportive for over ten years. From 1997 to 1998, Wang Zhusheng provided an academic home away from home at Yunnan University and facilitated my field research in Sipsongpanna. The field of anthropology was left poorer when he passed away in 1998. I remain grateful to my teacher at Wat Pajay, Dubi Sing (now Khanan Sing), for his assistance.

Many thanks to everyone at Columbia University Press, especially to editor Anne Routon for her buoyant enthusiasm. Wilson Wong performed arduous work in taking many of the photographs, and John Emerson helped with the maps.

I was lucky to get a lot of practice at a young age listening to skilled epic narrators. Thanks to my international family—especially my brother Sam—for great food, great stories, and even better senses of humor.

Finally, a toast to three companions in Jinghong: Rebecca Hampson, Zhou Yu, and Mat Matthewson. When life in Jinghong took a turn for the worse, Mat packed up his satchel, got on a bus, and left to seek greener pastures. Mat, wherever you are, cheers.

Map 1 Sipsongpanna (Xishuangbanna), Yunnan, China.

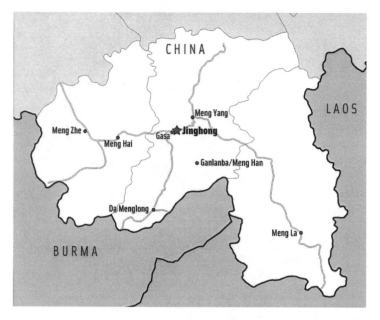

Map 2 Major Tai Lüe cities in the Mekong Delta.

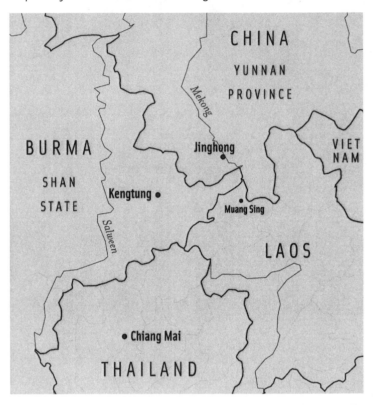

Song and
Silence

Introduction
The Writing on the Wall

The teak pillars that held up the eaves of the high temple roof outside had begun to bend and bow under its weight. Inside, the main hall of the temple was a dark forest of red lacquered pillars and handmade cotton streamers twirling below rafters that let in a few shafts of light and air. This temple, said to be the oldest still standing in the region, sat in an impoverished mountain village about an hour's drive from China's border with Burma.[1] The crude wooden Buddha statue seated on the dais, partially hidden between the pillars, was painted a cheap and sunny yellow where a wealthier village would have painted him gold. A few bundles of dried flowers on the ground before the statue testified to both the piety and the poverty of the villagers. Shutters hung askew at a square window, and an empty wooden bowl lay on the sill, collecting dust.

This temple was far off the beaten track, and I'd found it through a series of chances. While conducting research into the oral storytelling of Tai Lües in this region of southwest China, Sipsongpanna, I'd come across a fascinating Chinese essay describing the fine drawings in narrative Buddhist murals that depicted local legends. The article especially praised the old murals in temples in the west, near the Burmese border. I developed a thirst to see these and spent a week hopping buses along back roads, using the article as a guide. But though I spent long hours on local buses crammed between villagers and their bags of rice, and a few nights under the musty mosquito nets of old government guesthouses, I couldn't find a single old mural. A few temples had crude murals, clearly new, probably painted by monks who had returned from studies in northern Thailand: series of panels showing princes, ladies, golden spirits, and giant birds, all captioned with the looping Tai Lüe alphabet.

But the old murals, the ones described in the article, were hard to find. In some cases, when I read aloud the name of a temple from the article, local villagers shook their heads—they had never heard of it. Perhaps I mispronounced the name: Chinese and Tai Lüe are very different languages, and the written Chinese appellation gave few clues to the local name. Perhaps the old temples were gone, destroyed in World War II or during one of China's many political campaigns. Or perhaps the article had simply gotten it wrong: quite a few Chinese essays on ethnic minorities, I was learning, were written by scholars who had not studied in the region—or, as one Tai Lüe put it, "They sit in the library copying from one book into another, but never come to our Sipsongpanna."

While looking for the murals, though, I spoke with a lot of monks. Leaning against the railing of his temple porch, one husky, square-faced monk in Meng Zhe mentioned in passing that a nearby village housed the oldest temple in Sipsongpanna, and that it had not been touched since the seventeenth century.

I and a few Tai Lüe and Han Chinese friends who were also curious returned a few weeks later for a look. We hitched a ride on a local truck heading in the right direction and hopped off in the recommended village in late morning. It was empty—all of the adults and many of the children were no doubt working in the fields at the height of the busy season (see fig. 1 and fig. 2). The morning sunlight shone on grain spread out in the temple courtyard to dry. As we walked around the temple building, a cluster of barefoot village boys and a few small novice monks in tattered cotton robes came to watch us. They stood with their arms around each other, whispering and staring. "*Haw hoa leung*," one boy shouted in Tai Lüe, as the others giggled at the name he had called me: yellow-haired Han Chinese.

The temple was decrepit, and it certainly looked old, but there was no way to estimate its age. Peering at the outer walls, I began to

1 *Tai Lüe woman picking tea leaves.* PHOTO COURTESY OF WILSON WONG

2 *Tai Lüe girl carrying water.*   PHOTO COURTESY OF WILSON WONG

notice places where old murals had been carefully but incompletely scraped off. Old and delicate lines appeared on some areas of the white walls—the contour of a woman's face, the silhouette of a palace roof, a swirl of black ink. In a few places these were obscured by something painted in broad strokes of red, but this red paint had also been scraped off.

"Why did people scrape off the murals?" I asked the boys.

They pointed to the back of the temple. Here were a few places where the red paint had been left intact, forming old slogans (fig. 3). These read "Long Live Chairman Mao" and

> Any counterrevolutionary thing, if you do not knock it down, will not collapse of its own accord. This is like sweeping the ground: if the broom does not reach the dust, the dust will not usually go away of its own accord.

The boys took us up the hill at the top of the town to meet the *bawchang*, the layman in charge of temple affairs and record keeping

3 Cultural Revolution slogans on a temple wall.   PHOTO COURTESY OF WILSON WONG

(fig. 4). The wiry, elderly man, like many older villagers across China, still wore his blue Mao suit and cap. He sat us down and gave us tea. During China's Cultural Revolution (1966–1976), he said, Red Guards had descended on the village to knock down old buildings, destroy texts written in the Tai Lüe language, and burn the old, gold-covered image of the Buddha. He had convinced them not to knock the temple down by arguing that villagers used the building to store farm tools and grain. The Red Guards let the temple stand but scraped off the old Buddhist murals, replacing them with Maoist slogans. After the Cultural Revolution ended, the villagers carved and painted a new wooden Buddha statue and scraped off the desecrating slogans. But they left a few slogans up, he said, so that they wouldn't forget.

Was it true that the temple had not been altered for three hundred years? we asked. This seemed unlikely. The *bawchang* went to a trunk in his room and pulled out the parchment temple records marked in the spidery circles and half-moons of the old Tai Lüe script. Yes, he said, according to this, the last alterations were made in the late 1600s.

4 *Lay caretaker in front of the temple he protected from the Red Guards.*

* * *

THIS BOOK IS set mostly in quiet, subtropical Sipsongpanna (in Chinese, "Xishuangbanna"), an ethnic region that lies on China's borders with Burma and Laos. I lived in Jinghong, its capital, from 1997 to 1998 while conducting doctoral research on Tai Lüe *changkhap* ("skilled chant" or "skilled chanters"), a term used for professionally trained oral poets and the narrative poetry they compose and perform. Eventually it seemed impossible to understand the narrative poems outside of the modernizing, changing context in which they were performed. However, that context wasn't simple; it was a divided and contentious one. Like the layers of paint and the scrapings on the temple walls, the series of political campaigns and tumultuous economic changes in the region had left their marks.

There seemed to be two separate and distinct Tai Lüe cultures in Sipsongpanna. As part of its expansion into the land on the national borders and its appropriation of material resources there (gold, minerals, teak, and so on), the Chinese state had engaged in explicit projects to create a national culture and to identify, categorize, and shape the identities of the nation's fifty-six officially recognized *minzu* ("nationalities"). These nationalities marked out the limits of allowable ethnic self-expression in China, and ethnic minorities, like the Tai Lüe, who participate in state displays and self-commodification for tourism, are rewarded with official praise and economic wealth. To challenge those limits by insisting on other kinds of language or religion, as ethnic Tibetans, Uyghurs, and Inner Mongolians sometimes do, is to risk violent conflict with the state.

But in Sipsongpanna, some elements of the unapproved, unofficial ethnic culture were also preserved underground. An ancient text, an old temple, an epic poem in praise of the dead prince: all were saved because someone took a risk; hid them in the rafters of a stilt house; persuaded the Red Guards to pass them over; sang them to a listening student at night. Much was also saved because Sipsongpanna is laced with a web of forest paths that connect it to related peoples in nearby Southeast Asia. When war or political campaigns roiled one Tai region, residents could smuggle children, texts, and songs across the borders to be kept by cousins for a few years.

As I followed my search for oral storytellers in Sipsongpanna, I found a growing ethnic revival movement emerging piecemeal below the radar of the state. During the past ten years, young Tai Lüe monks and activists have created a grassroots movement that spans national borders, drawing on contacts and exchange with related parts of Thailand, Burma, and Laos. They have revived indigenous Tai Lüe Buddhism, building hundreds of temples and initiating thousands of Buddhist novices. They have used new technology, such as Macintosh computers bought in Thailand, and pop and rock music learned from Tais in Burma, to interest youth in their own language and culture. And young people are also learning how to perform old oral narratives. They do much of this behind the scenes, hidden from the direct gaze of the state and the competing show put on for tourists. They also have ongoing and sometimes heated debates about how best to move forward, and they discuss which cultural style, artifact, song, language, or temple truly represents "real Tai culture."

Thus while many Tai Lües participate agreeably in the public showcasing of their ethnic identity staged by the Chinese state—to such a degree that they are sometimes portrayed as a "model minority" in Chinese official media—they live in a different world by night. Tai Lües have avoided open conflict and managed a boundary between the public and private spheres.

A book published in the United States about any part of that private culture risks testing those limits. The question that haunted some people in Sipsongpanna now faces me: If they tell me and I publish the name of the village that holds the oldest temple in the region, what will happen to it? Will it be knocked down, rebuilt, and marketed as a tourist attraction, or allowed to continue quietly rotting? Will a book that makes hidden things visible make life better or worse for those who risked everything to keep a temple, a book, or a song? This book includes many of their songs, but under the circumstances it is not surprising that some Tai Lües chose silence.

Before turning to these issues, this chapter introduces some basic facts about the region. It also gives a brief view of China's history since 1949, focusing on the state's very conscious invention of a new national culture in the early twentieth century and its equally conscious invention of ethnic minority identities. Readers familiar with this background may wish to skip ahead to the following chapters.

Sipsongpanna

ETHNIC MINORITY GROUPS that once had semi-independent states occupy China's national borders and most of its arable land. Sipsongpanna is one of the smallest such regions, but because of a tourist boom in the late 1990s it is one of the best known within China.

Xishuangbanna Dai Nationality Autonomous Prefecture ("Xishuangbanna Daizu zizhizhou") lies on the southern tip of China's Yunnan province, on the borders of Burma and Laos. The subtropical, mountainous region covers about 7,400 square miles. Sipsongpanna's contemporary name comes from a sixteenth-century Tai Lüe name, Muang Sipsongpanna, which literally means "the city-state of twelve townships" ("*sipsong*" means twelve, "*panna*" means village rice field or township). In the past it was sometimes also referred to by Tais as Muang Balanasi, a place name derived from the legend of the Buddha.[2] Administratively, Xishuangbanna is divided into three counties: Jinghong county, with Jinghong as the prefectural capital; Meng Hai county to the west, bordering on Burma; and Meng La county to the east, bordering on Laos (see map 1).

The region has an ethnically diverse population of roughly one million. Over a third are Tai Lüe, another third are Han Chinese, and the last third are made up of a number of other ethnic minorities. These include the variously named Akha (in Chinese, "Aini" or "Hani"), Blang (in Chinese, "Bulang"), Karen (in Chinese, "Jinuo"), Wa, Yao, Hmong (in Chinese, "Miao"), Lahu, Khmu, and others. Official counts of the number of ethnic groups in Sipsongpanna range from thirteen to sixteen.

But Chinese Tai Lües claim closer kinship with the many related Tai groups—in Vietnam, Laos, Thailand, Burma, and Assam, India—that collectively make up part of the "Tai-Kadai" language family. Tai peoples form a ribbon across India, China, and Southeast Asia and share elements of one another's cultures, religious beliefs, and social customs. Tai Lües of Sipsongpanna are closest to Tai Khuns of Kengtung, Shan State, Burma. They also have close linguistic, cultural, and economic ties with Tais in Muang Sing, Laos, and residents of northern and northeastern Thailand (see map 2). The mountainous borders between these countries are difficult to police, and in some areas it is possible to cross the border without knowing it.

The prefecture (in Chinese, "*zhou*") has the three seasons typical in much of mainland Southeast Asia: a temperate winter, from October to February; a hot season, from February to June; and a rainy season, from June to September, known as "*Vasaa*," the Buddhist retreat period. Most Tai Lües are valley dwellers and rice farmers, and the region's main products are rice, rubber, tropical fruits, and green tea. The Chinese practice of drinking tea, in fact, derives from medieval (ca. seventh century) Han contact and trade with peoples in this region, and pungent tea from the mountainous area near Meng Hai, known as "*nuomi xiangcha*" in Chinese, is popular throughout China. Sipsongpanna boasted impressive biodiversity, but hunting and the logging of the rainforest as well as deforestation for some ill-conceived economic development projects such as rubber farming have eradicated much local flora and fauna, including wild tigers, buffalo, and many birds. In recent years, some efforts at environmental preservation have begun to bring back some of the native birds and trees.

Most Tai Lües live in villages outside of Jinghong, usually in large, spacious wooden or bamboo stilt houses, passed through the family from mother to youngest daughter. The stilt houses have high roofs and three main areas: living room, bedroom, and kitchen. A large open communal space with wicker sofas, low stools, and a television/karaoke set usually also has stacks of cotton mattresses and small wicker tables that enable a family to entertain dozens of guests at a moment's notice. There are also a private, off-limits communal family bedroom and a covered porch, which is both the kitchen and washroom. Animals, farm tools, tractors, and bicycles are housed below, and well-to-do families sometimes build toilets in this area underneath the house (but karaoke machines are more common than toilets). Traditionally, monks do not walk underneath houses because other people may then be walking over their heads, which are considered sacred.

The houses tend to be built closely enough to one another that neighbors can converse from their porches. A web of well-swept dirt paths and a shared network of fishponds and streams connect them. Many backyards have fruit trees, and farmers returning from the field may spend the afternoon picking fruit. Bamboo is important: Sipsongpanna has hundreds of varieties, and these are used to make most tools and toys for children. Tai Lüe villages are usually situated in valleys, and rice is the main crop. Farmers use water buffalo for rice cultivation and slaughter them to provide meat for major celebrations, such as a monk ordination. They raise pigs and fowl for meat and eggs.

Tai Lüe cuisine is highly varied, favoring hot and sour flavors. A typical Tai Lüe meal is a spread of dozens of bowls containing fried meats, raw and steamed wild vegetables and bamboos, and spicy *nami*—dips made with tomatoes, olives, or peanuts as a base. These dishes are tasted with handfuls of *khao nua*, sticky rice dipped in the sauces by hand. On holidays, sticky rice is made into a paste sweetened with mashed banana and wrapped in banana leaves as a gift to others. Rice is used to make *lao*, a peppery alcohol brewed in barrels and drunk in shots.

Before what the Chinese Communist Party refers to as its "liberation" of Sipsongpanna in 1953, Tai Lües here formed a small kingdom that was partially colonized by a series of Chinese empires but that from day-to-day was largely left to run itself and to form its own alliances with neighboring states.[3] After so-called liberation, contacts with those across the new Chinese borders were restricted. Projects aiming to reform land ownership, political systems, agriculture, education, and local culture, all run by Beijing, created a new sense of Tai Lües as subordinates within the new nation. Minorities like the Tai Lüe benefited by receiving electricity, medical care, new roads, and other improvements. But while comrades, they were always junior comrades, "little brother minorities."

The Need for Unification

WITHIN CHINA THE Tai Lüe are called *"Daizu"* or "Dai nationality," a group that includes a branch of the Tai Neua who live in the Dehong region of western Yunnan province, as well as others scattered in smaller numbers throughout Yunnan.[4] Historically, mostly because of the geographical obstacles and distances involved, Dehong and Sipsongpanna had little contact with each other, compared to the contact each had with nearby kingdoms in modern-day Burma. The Sipsongpanna and Dehong Tai spoken languages and writing systems are related, but they are not mutually comprehensible. This relatively recently invented ethnic identity, and the cultural productions[5] related to it, were the product of two related processes: the creation of a national Chinese culture and the categorization of ethnic groups as part of the new nation-state.

In 1949, having won a long civil war, the leaders of the new People's Republic of China faced a highly fragmented country. The remains of the last dynasty, the Qing, had been split into bits by half a century of chaos. Warlords had ruled China for decades, and because there had never been national education or anything like a national media, the country was a patchwork of localities with diverse languages, cultures, and customs. In much of the country, residents of one town could not understand those in the next one.

Moreover, while the new leaders aimed to reclaim the land that had belonged to the last imperial dynasty, the presence of semi-independent ethnic peoples all around the borders posed an obstacle. Roughly 60 percent of the new nation's landmass was occupied by 10 percent of its population. As Ma Yin succinctly observes:

> Minority nationalities live in places with the following common characteristics:
>
> 1) A wide expanse of land with a sparse distribution of population. Many minority peoples have traditionally established their villages in mountains and pastoral areas, on high plateaus and in deep forests.
> 2) A wide range of products and abundant mineral resources.
> 3) Strategically important as border regions for the whole country.[6]

Security was an especially urgent concern. While these resource-rich, land-rich, and potentially disloyal ethnic peoples sat on the borders, vanquished troops were gathering nearby. Sometimes funded and trained by the United States and other Western countries, they were launching periodic guerrilla attacks on the weakest points of the new socialist state.[7]

It was urgently necessary to simplify the complex problems of loyalty and territoriality posed by the chaos of the whole nation and in particular to bring those open, fluid borders under control. To do this, China's new leaders developed a number of new policies and projects, including two that are especially relevant for this book: they set out to create a new, popular national culture and to bring ethnic minorities into the national fold.

Scripts and States

IN *IMAGINED COMMUNITIES*, Benedict Anderson argues that empires were socially imagined through the "medium of a sacred language and written script."[8] He singles out China as an example, observing that the Chinese empire and other "great classical communities conceived of themselves as cosmically central, through the medium of a sacred language linked to a superterrestrial order of power."[9] The sacred language or writing system was preserved in a "high center," fading out to "porous and indistinct" borders. Nations, says Anderson, differentiate themselves from empires because they are unified through a vernacular printed language that is equally accessible to all. The simultaneous consumption of narratives such as novels and newspapers helps to create the national ideal of horizontal comradeship. Thus, scripts and printed texts help to build the power of both empires and nation-states.

As Anderson surmises, political power in imperial China was in fact predicated on mastery of an arcane written language known as "*wenyan*," which was used by officials and impenetrable to anyone who had not been carefully trained in it. Had the elite class set out to invent a written code that would obscure the workings of power, they could hardly have done better. Young men from good families were trained in wenyan and the Confucian canon by private tutors; for much of Chinese history, few others had access to education. In order to climb the ranks of the government bureaucracy, men had to prove their mastery of the canon in a civil service exam that tested not one's capacity to govern but one's ability to write and quote literature. Those who were not literate in wenyan were seen by these literary elites as something less than fully human.

This bureaucratic system, predicated on an arcane written code, inevitably created a tightly controlled and elite literary culture that Victor Mair calls the "culture of the capital." China's imperial traditions of literature, philosophy, and painting are internationally renowned for their refined and elaborate character, but Mair says the "culture of the capital" was so hegemonic and closed that it virtually erased noncanonical, regional culture:

One suspects—indeed, one is certain—that much of Chinese culture that was of great worth has been irretrievably destroyed simply because it did not fit the mold of officialdom. To gain some idea of the magnitude of our loss, all we need do is think of the texts that have been recovered from the deserts of Central Asia and temple libraries of Japan during the past century.[10]

This "culture of the capital" was exported to the borders and colonies through what Stevan Harrell calls the empire's "civilizing project," in which the inequality between the civilizing center and the peripheral peoples has its ideological basis in the center's claim to a superior degree of civilization, along with a commitment to raise the peripheral peoples' civilization to the level of the center, or at least closer to that level.[11]

Civilizing projects, says Harrell, characterized Chinese imperial relations with the southwest borders, the nineteenth-century relations of Western Christian missionaries with the same region, and the central planning and policies that followed China's incorporation of the region in 1949.[12]

Throughout its history, China certainly had a rich and vibrant professional oral culture. Most members of the elite class enjoyed slipping off to listen to the many genres of oral literature—Beijing drumsongs ("*dagu*"), lyrical strumming odes ("*tanci*"), speed stories ("*kuai shu*"), and clapper songs (in Cantonese, "*muk'yu*")—performed by trained, professional oral poets and singers. But as Mair points out, the educated elite class publicly disparaged this kind of oral poetry and drama, especially oral literature in local dialects or minority languages. The only true literature was written literature. Elite texts literally propped up the empire, and relatively little of China's rich oral and popular cultures was recorded for posterity.

The May Fourth Movement

THE REVOLUTION THAT laid the foundation for China's emergence as a modern nation-state in the early twentieth century began with literary and linguistic reformers who drew on the country's folklore to challenge the literary canon. This movement threw out wenyan and replaced it with *baihua*, the spoken Chinese vernacular; they threw out the old Confucian canon and created new fiction and poetry written for ordinary readers. The May Fourth Movement officially began on May 4, 1919, when Beijing University students led a mass street demonstration to protest the government's ceding German colonial possessions in China to Japan. The protest spread like wildfire to other Chinese cities, igniting a series of nationalist demonstrations, strikes, and protests by young women and men. But as with all such mass movements, the groundwork had been laid over previous years, with the publication of hundreds of new journals, magazines, and newspapers and the formation of discussion groups that explored national identity and culture.

The leaders of this movement were thinkers and writers, including many who had been educated abroad. They included author Lu Xun, who wrote masterful works of fiction lampooning Confucianism,[13] and Chen Duxiu, who founded the prominent journal *Xin qingnian* (New youth) and, later, the Chinese Communist Party. Chen argued that to establish a "modern Western nation" China needed true equality, which was not compatible with its old Confucian traditions; these must be destroyed, he said, to make way for new ideals.[14] The writer Hu Shi proclaimed that literary Chinese was a dead language and became the leading advocate of language reform. These writers grew excited about the idea of creating a living, popular Chinese literature by researching their own folk and oral traditions and drawing new vitality from them.

The new ideas rapidly took hold. In 1918, Beijing University scholars established an office for folk song studies and established a journal to publish them. By 1920, the Ministry of Education decreed that primary schools should teach only from books written in the vernacular.[15] Soon, many journals and newspapers were publishing text in the vernacular, including newly unearthed folk songs. Some scholars began to do field research: across the country, intellectuals went into villages that had long been viewed as cultural wastelands by educated elites and there recorded some of the rich regional oral literature. Meanwhile, others argued that the road to the future lay in imitating the West. At this stage, the question, "What is a real Chinese culture?" had as many answers as there were writers and thinkers in China. The Japanese invasion, World War II, and China's civil war interrupted the debate.

As the war ground to a close, the victorious Chinese Communist Party reduced the many contesting answers to the question of Chinese identity to one. As summarized by Mao Zedong in the *Talks at the Yenan Forum on Literature and Art*:

Life as reflected in works of literature and art can and ought to be on a higher plane, more intense, more concentrated, more typical, nearer the ideal, and therefore more universal than actual everyday life. Revolutionary literature and art should create a variety of characters out of real life and help the masses propel history forward.[16]

In order to create works that would unite the people "with one heart and one mind," Mao said, writers and artists should

go among the masses; they must for a long period of time unreservedly and whole-heartedly go into the heat of the struggle, go to the only source, the broadest and richest source, in order to observe, experience, study and analyze . . . all the raw materials of literature and art.[17]

But for an artist, the task was anything but clear. Having gone whole-heartedly among the masses, what was one supposed to return with? The safest answer seemed to be their folklore, turned into politically approved texts. Thus, newly formed culture committees launched a major effort to document rural Chinese folktales, songs, dances, and proverbs, publishing volumes that presented the results.

This new reading public, which spoke hundreds of diverse Chinese languages,[18] was gradually being unified by books and magazines publishing folklore texts in the official vernacular and by a new, more accessible "simplified script" (*jianti zi*) invented by government committees of linguists. The simplified characters would replace the unstandardized old Chinese characters, and, linguists argued, since fewer strokes were used to write them, the simplified script would be easier to learn and remember and thus promote wider literacy.

Under the classical "culture of the capital," ethnic peoples were doubly marginalized because they were both ethnically different and predominantly nonliterate. Anderson says that nations distinguish themselves from empires because nations replace "high centers" with "horizontal comradeships." But this horizontal comradeship can become a hegemonic fraternity when faced with ethnic and linguistic difference. In the process of creating new texts—maps, books, song lyrics—states create a script that undergirds political authority, but in the process it displaces and marginalizes other forms of expression. This began to happen in China as the new nation-state used its new scripts, texts, and maps to domesticate the ethnic borderlands.

Ethnic Classification

WHILE FIGHTING THE revolution, the Chinese Communist Party had promised the ethnic minorities who assisted them (such as the Tai Lüe) self-determination, regional autonomy, and the right to secede. But having achieved power, the Party withdrew the promised right to secession and instead began to speak of the importance of Beijing's help in overcoming ethnic "backwardness." Newly "autonomous regions" were established for ethnic minorities, but autonomy was always to be subject to the leadership of the Party and through it, Beijing. Local Party representatives delivered instructions to ethnic leaders and approved their decisions. But now the Party faced the problem of political representation for the ethnic groups at the national level. As China's foremost anthropologist, Fei Xiaotong, wrote, the new People's Republic was committed to ethnic equality on the one hand, but, on the other hand,

> the principle would have been meaningless without proper recognition of existing nationalities. For how could a People's Congress allocate its seats to deputies from different nationalities without knowing what nationalities there were? And how could the nation effect regional autonomy for the nationalities without a clear idea of their geographical distribution?[19]

The state invited ethnic minorities to come forward and self-identify as distinct groups. In 1955, Fei tells us, over 400 different ethnic groups registered, 260 of them in Yunnan.[20] This created what, in retrospect, sounds like panic in Beijing; tribesmen would overrun the majority Han Chinese government. Ethnic identity had to be simplified.

To do this, China launched a massive research project in "ethnic identification." In 1953, the government dispatched teams of ethnographers to border regions containing minority peoples. These researchers spent years collecting data on ethnic politics, institutions, agriculture, myth, and language. Ethnographers categorized groups as ethnic nationalities based on Stalin's criteria of nationalities as defined by shared language, territory, and "psychology." They also placed the new nationalities on a social-evolutionary scale, drawing from Marxist theory and from the work of American anthropologist Lewis Henry Morgan; inevitably, nationalities were placed on the lower rungs of the evolutionary hierarchy, while the majority Hans were placed on the top. The end result was a comprehensive list of fifty-five minority nationalities, folding some of the original 400 back into the Han and melding together some (such as the Tai Lüe and Tai Neua, now both named "Dai") that had previously had little or no contact. Fifty-five was apparently a more manageable number of groups than 400, and folklore had emerged as a catchall answer to several questions about how best to unify the new nation.

Ethnographic study teams then produced reports summarizing everything there was to know about each ethnic minority group.[21] Subsequent books popularized the information gathered in these reports. Typical examples presented short overviews of Dais adorned with illustrations of women singing and dancing, women performing the famous "peacock dance," and Buddhist reliquaries and palm trees. The books described the Dai minority as a tiny group exclusive to China, without reference to the links with related kingdoms across the borders. They referred to Dai feudalism and slavery, "primitive spirit worship," and the much vaunted (though factually inaccurate) "freedom of young men and women" to practice "free love."[22] Summarizing their expressive culture, Ma Yin comments, "they love to sing and dance."[23] Based on this description, Dais were categorized as a feudal society and as slave-owners, placing them somewhere above the "cannibalistic" Wa and below the majority Han. For the most part, these reports and books, which remain the authoritative sources on ethnic minorities in China to this day, solidified the position of ethnic minorities at the bottom of a social-evolutionary hierarchy within the Chinese nation. Some social scientists, such as Fei Xiaotong, took a more nuanced view of ethnic identity, but many others codified misunderstandings and stereotypes and used them to justify an ethnocentric hierarchy that became the basis of state policy. In addition, researchers produced numerous volumes of ethnic minority folktales and songs, discussed in more detail in subsequent chapters.

With ethnic minorities labeled as backward and primitive in so many respects, ethnic folklore became just one of the many aspects of these groups that needed improving and modernizing under the leadership of the Party. Researchers and government culture bureau officials explicitly encouraged and promoted elements of minority culture deemed positive, socialist, and modern, while carefully pruning elements deemed counterproductive, counterrevolutionary, or primitive. For instance, traditional minority clothing was a positive expression of ethnic identity, to be celebrated and promoted. Minority religious rituals, however, were counterrevolutionary and economically wasteful, and as such were discouraged. Dances and oral literature were studied and in some cases "improved" by state choreographers and authors—a process discussed in more detail in following chapters.

To lead the cultural aspects of this improvement project, the government established a number of state organs: "the development and flourishing of minority nationality literature and art will essentially rely on government organizations to manage it, and on the leadership and assistance of the nation."[24] The state set up culture bureaus in each ethnic region and at the provincial level to manage the nationalities' song-and-dance troupes. In addition to the culture bureaus, the government established local government-run news media in minority regions to broadcast news in minority languages.

Much of the new cultural production by the state revolved around the management of language, and government language policy became one of the most contentious issues in ethnic regions. National autonomy laws guaranteed minorities the right to education, media, and publishing in ethnic languages.[25] In practice, in many regions publications and broadcasts in the local minority language were so minimal and inept as to suggest that what the government really aimed to do was to phase them out and replace them with Chinese. In Sipsongpanna in the late 1990s there were a one-hour weekly television news broadcast in Tai Lüe and a daily radio hour playing folk recordings of oral poetry; most of the rest of the television and radio programming was in Chinese. A local newspaper, the *Xishuangbanna bao* (Sipsongpanna times), printed four to eight pages of officially approved news per week, most of it translations of official news from Beijing that had already appeared in the Chinese-language papers. But in fact this was not printed in the Tai Lüe script that had been used in Sipsongpanna for centuries. Instead, the government intervened and created a "new Dai script," a simplified alphabet aimed to promote wider literacy in the region. As later chapters will show, this turned out to be one of the most controversial government interventions into Tai Lüe culture.

The Cultural Revolution

UP UNTIL THE early to mid-1960s, the new national government made a commitment to supporting and developing ethnic culture—even if it was only the cultural forms that fit into the new, official ethnic identities or that had been shaped to fit them. All this was disrupted during the Cultural Revolution. The movement to "Destroy the Four Olds and Establish the Four News" began in Beijing in August 1966 and quickly fanned out to rural areas. While it had a devastating impact on all of China, the effects in ethnic minority regions may have been worst; of course, this is difficult to judge, as ethnic minorities are often still afraid to discuss it.

Red Guards in many areas of China confiscated Buddhist icons, sutras, and religious treasures, destroyed Buddhist relics, pillaged temples, and compelled monks to defrock. Ethnic minorities were told that their period of adaptation to the new nation had ended and that they were expected instantly and fully to assimilate into the majority Han Chinese nation. Many minority groups changed their traditional holidays or altered ethnic-sounding names to make them more "revolutionary."[26] Abbots and others who protested were jailed. In Sipsongpanna, Tai temples and reliquaries were destroyed, sacred sites desecrated, sutra texts seized, and images of the Buddha publicly burned. Sacred forests, believed to be the homes of Tai Lüe spirits and ancestors, were cut down. Many people, especially monks and their families, fled over the borders to Laos and Thailand. Old Tai Lüe texts were seized and removed from Sipsongpanna by Red Guards and officials and were probably destroyed. A few former monks hid books and scriptures in the rafters of their homes or buried them in the forests.

As one Tai Lüe man in his thirties put it, "We Tais have lost a generation. It will take many generations to build our culture up again to where it was before the Cultural Revolution." Such feelings about the Cultural Revolution are common throughout China, but they may have an added bitterness in ethnic regions, where despite the active involvement of minorities in the actual events, the Cultural Revolution is viewed as a movement that came from Beijing and that continued earlier Han projects of domination.

As Erik Mueggler notes regarding another ethnic region of Yunnan, "memories of past violence are crucial to people's sense of their own relation to distant centers of state power."[27] The scars left by the Cultural Revolution were sometimes as visible as the scrapings on the murals and the slogans on the temple wall.

China certainly has left the Cultural Revolution behind, but ethnic minorities are aware that the state's tolerance of their cultures and religions still runs hot and cold. The slogans left on the temple wall are not just a memorial to past trauma but a warning of present dangers. Most Tais are well aware that demands by Tibetan Buddhists and Muslim Uyghurs in northwest Xinjiang for basic religious, linguistic, and cultural rights continue to result in brutal crackdowns, long jail sentences, torture, and summary execution.[28] While I spoke with monks about the revival of ethnic education in Sipsongpanna, Uyghur mosques and schools were being closed in Xinjiang. While Tai Lüe activists were promoting the use of their language and raising concerns about the loss of the rainforests, Tibetan monks who advocated the use of their traditional language and protested deforestation were being beaten and jailed. From 1998 through 2000, the nationwide crackdown on the Chinese meditation group Falun Gong reached into Sipsongpanna. Practitioners were jailed, and Tai Lüe Buddhist monks were compelled to sit through long political indoctrination sessions.

In the years after the end of the Cultural Revolution, central planners took a new tack in border regions. The new leadership embraced economic development. International backpackers had been traveling to small towns in Yunnan for years, and perhaps because of this early success Sipsongpanna and other Yunnan regions were chosen for the targeted development of a national tourism industry. But with Sipsongpanna's state-inspired tourism boom also came waves of new migrants: Han Chinese from other rural areas and sometimes from the cities looking for new economic opportunities. In 1999, Mette Halskov Hansen reported that while Hans made up less than one-third of the population of Sipsongpanna, they made up 48 percent of the residents in Jinghong, the region's capital. She adds, "since only those who are registered as having permanently moved to Sipsong Panna are counted in these statistics the actual proportion of Han Chinese is considerably higher."[29] The new migrants had Chinese-language skills, education, and capital that made them stronger competitors than local minorities for jobs and businesses serving the tourist market. They brought with them a flood of Chinese-language music, books, films, and culture that dwarfed the meager local government productions in Tai Lüe language. While some embraced the change, other ethnic minorities began to fear total assimilation into the Han Chinese mainstream.

This brings us to 1997, when this book begins. In the first chapter, we see the "front stage": the view of Sipsongpanna presented to tourists and the limits of ethnic expression allowed by the state. The second chapter ventures into the "backstage" sphere, where Tai Lües are reviving old Buddhist traditions, borrowing new technology, inventing pop music in their language, crossing national borders, and finding ways to resist state control of their culture without engaging in open confrontation.

The third chapter recounts an interview with a legendary Tai Lüe oral poet and takes his life as a prism through which to view the state's conquest of oral and textual traditions through a "simplifying project" that shaped ethnic culture, creating the front-stage sphere. The fourth chapter charts the revival of oral traditions as part of the Buddhist movement.

The final chapter travels overland into Burma to explore how the Chinese state's intervention in ethnic culture paved the roads that gave Chinese officials and entrepreneurs access to material resources in both China and Burma. In the midst of a struggle over resources on both sides of the border, Buddhist temples have become sites of quiet contest between the front-stage and backstage spheres, and thus between governments and ethnic minorities in both countries.

A Note on Methods

IN EMBARKING TOGETHER on this research project, my Sipsongpanna hosts and I found ourselves straining against the history of how other "outside people" (as Tai Lües refer to everyone not from Sipsongpanna) have studied minorities in China. During the year I spent trying to convince informants to let me do things in my "right" way, I was taught their "right" way, and the two were not always the same. My way of doing fieldwork, shaped by colonial and postcolonial Western ethnographic methods, was to be a "participant observer," to study Tai Lüe, take copious notes, and spend what often seemed to my local colleagues to be unnecessary amounts of time in the careful recording, transcription, and translation of song texts.

My colleagues' way, learned over decades of experience as the subject of dozens of research trips by ethnographers seeking to categorize them, was to treat visitors as people of high rank, feeding them at formal banquets, introducing them to prestigious people, educating them with long, formal speeches, and keeping them away from the rituals, ceremonies, and songs that Tai Lües performed for themselves. Early on, my requests for interviews were almost always met with ceremonious gifts, such as offerings of books in Chinese. While my slower, laborious, and frankly nosy approach was sometimes tiresome to my hosts, some Tai Lües felt that their local culture had not been adequately appreciated or supported by the state and saw my research as confirming this claim. For others, my presence became a way to have conversations about larger political issues with one another.

To protect local people in China and Burma from political repercussions for their frankness, I've changed their names and some other identifying characteristics. The exceptions to this rule are the Tai Lüe singers and oral poets, who wished for their names and work be recognized.

All these factors, and others as well, shaped the book that follows.

1

Front Stage

The plane dipped and began its descent, sweeping over a sea of green whorls, the tea bushes that curved over Sipsongpanna's rolling hills. Trails of mist rose off the muddy, turgid Mekong as it snaked between them. The plane flew low, skimming over women in baggy clothes hunched over tea plants with sagging cotton shoulder bags. Our cabin was packed with groups of elated Chinese businessmen, smiling and leaning against the plane's portholes as they posed for photos. *Women qu kaihui*, explained the suited man in the next seat: We're going for a conference.

Coming out of the plane's door onto a shaky stairway on wheels, we were hit by a wall of warm air, fragrant with the green rot of the surrounding rice fields. The airport was new, and just beyond the barbed wire fence of the landing strip women and children waded, pants rolled knee high, into the spiky muck, working with bunches of rice. The airport had a high-spirited, slapdash atmosphere. Small trucks wheeled giddily, piled pell-mell with cheap plastic suitcases, and dark men in blue jumpsuits lounged in the doorways, smoking, watching us, and laughing. A few bored-looking young women in polyester sarongs and heavy makeup stood by the glass doorways, splashing water at us and striking gongs. As we dragged our suitcases into the parking lot, the businessmen from the plane insisted that we all take a group photo. The airport employees locked up the building behind us, and I hauled my heavy suitcases onto the hotel bus bound for Jinghong town.

The one-lane road into town was packed with trucks piled with tree trunks from Burma, honking red taxicabs, and camouflage-green tractors. The bus lagged behind a *tuolaji*, a tractor driven by a man straddling the engine and holding its reins. A cluster of women in long sarongs and floppy straw hats and barefoot boys carrying cloth satchels over their shoulders stood behind him, hanging on and shouting laughingly over the sputtering engine. A farmer with a switch drove a group of muddy, dolorous oxen across the road. Both sides of the road were lined with wooden houses on stilts, ladders climbing to the main floors that had been turned into impromptu cafés to serve the truck and tractor drivers. Women in long skirts with elaborate hair buns leaned over the balconies of these houses and shouted jokes to the guys driving tractors. The cacophony was punctuated by the cries of roosters. Some of the cafés had signs with the Tai Lüe script of circles.

In no time we were in Jinghong, which was full of the white box buildings typical of any Chinese town but here shaded by rows of palm trees (fig. 5). People squatted on the stoops of storefronts or on bamboo stools in the street, smoking, talking, fixing bikes, and spitting. In 1918, an American Christian missionary, William Clifton Dodd, descended from his horse in Jinghong and called it "a sleepy old town on a magnificent site." He remarked on the thickness of the forest lining the river, writing, "little can be seen from the river excepting the numerous temples and the long sloping roof of the palace."[1] Eighty years later, the palace, temples, and trees were gone, and little could be seen of the river through a forest of concrete and tinted blue glass.

I booked a room at the government guesthouse, the Xishuangbanna Binguan, for roughly seven dollars a night for the next year, and hauled my huge bags up to the second floor, sweating, under the impassive gaze of the hotel *fuwuyuan* ("service personnel"). For the next several months they would bring daily thermoses of hot water, change my sheets, empty my wastebasket, listen in on my phone calls, gossip with and about my friends, and, no doubt, report on all of the above to the local public security bureau. The provincial-level PSB had approved my research proposal to study Tai Lüe folklore.

5 *Downtown Jinghong.*

The room had a white mosquito net hanging from the ceiling in a neat twist. There were a couple of tottering wicker chairs that I would later pull out to sit on the balcony during the long midday *xiuxi* ("afternoon siesta"). The clean-swept concrete floor was cool under my bare feet. A trail of steam rose from a heavy, dented red thermos of boiled water. Outside the window, in the courtyard below, an elderly man in a blue Mao suit and cap sat watch over a throng of battered bicycles for rent. After a brief burst of elation at having finally arrived, I sat down on the creaking bed and contemplated the stains on the wallpaper left by the previous year's monsoon.

Then I did what many people do when confronted with the new and overwhelming: I reached for an interpretive text. At the top of my suitcase was a fat red book that read "CHINA" on the cover and "Lonely Planet" on the spine, and under the entry "Yunnan-Jinghong" was a column headed "Places to eat." It advised, "As with accommodation, Manting Lu is the place for Dai-style food"[2] ("*lu*" is Chinese for road). A small map on the next page showed Manting Road—two lines running parallel to the Mekong River, beginning in the center of town and finishing at the edge of the page. The two lines were crowded with the symbols that promised a lively cluster of cafés, hotels, and bars. I dog-eared the page, slipped on a pair of flip-flops, picked up my hotel room key, and walked out to start on the first task of a year's research: to find Manting Road.

CHINA–Yunnan–Jinghong–Manting Road

IN WAYS THAT William Clifton Dodd might have had difficulty imagining, I had arrived in not one town, but two. There was one town for outsiders, visitors like me: the one on the map in the Lonely Planet guidebook, which marked towns, theme parks, famous temples, and invented tourist sights such as the "tree that looks like an elephant park." Texts, whether maps, guidebooks, histories, or literary canons, have shaped the politics of the border region in many ways.[3] The Lonely Planet's map had been copied and altered from an official government map for tourists, one that in Chinese and English marked Jinghong as a minor subcategory of the larger encompassing province, Yunnan; the province itself is a minor subcategory of the very large Chinese nation. Its incorporation at the bottom of the hierarchy of the Chinese state was an important reality of everyday life in Jinghong, and one reinforced by the ways that the state had chosen to reinvent the region for Chinese and foreign tourists.

Manting Road was a product of that reinvention for tourists, but as it turned out the road was also a fiction created by the Chinese map. Jinghong, I discovered, had another geography that was resistant and underground. This resistant geography had never been committed to paper but was kept alive in local language and culture. Over time, I came to see the areas on the tourist map as part of Jinghong's "front stage," and the places of that other unwritten geography as its "backstage."

These two conflicting geographies had not emerged overnight; historical forces of money and power had shaped the landscape. Through centuries of "civilizing projects" aimed at bringing elite Chinese imperial culture to the border peoples, local minorities had become largely acculturated to China and had learned how to present themselves in ways that Chinese officials would find appealing and acceptable. More recently, this self-presentation had been reinforced and capitalized through the economic development of tourism, which created ethnic theme parks, dance halls, and hotels, patronized mostly by Chinese tourists. National mass media and local government media had collectively created stereotyped images of smiling minorities. In ways that Beijing would approve of, local government authorities had constructed theme parks that took the list of nationality characteristics compiled in the 1950s and staged those characteristics as displays, turning them into elements of safe tourist playgrounds. In the private sector, which again was policed by local authorities, restaurant and hotel ethnic dance revues reenacted the same representations of ethnic culture. The end result of all this was an adult playground peopled with dancing ethnic women in tight sarongs, swaying palm trees, and exotic fruits and animals. It was sustained by a massive and illicit economy: the trade in sex, drugs, gambling, and smuggled goods.

But off the tourist map, in interstitial spaces emerging in temples and villages, Tai Lües were reviving historical relationships with other Tais across the borders and were building a grassroots movement aimed at reviving and reinventing traditional oral and Buddhist culture. The temple and village areas of Jinghong that were the centers of this resistant activity were located at the bottom of Manting Road. In moving from the top of Manting Road to the bottom, one moved from the Han-dominated center of town—close to the government compound and the big hotels—to a region dominated by Tai Lüe villages and the Buddhist temple. At its peak in the late 1990s, the street linked the pan-Tai, fluid, cross-border network of the Mekong Delta with the bounded, categorized, and hierarchical system of the Chinese nation-state. In many ways, the spectrum of cultural expression and debate one could hear along Manting Road pointed to a fault line running below the region.

Tourism Development

IN THE FEVER of planning that seized official China during the first decades after the end of the Cultural Revolution, the national government decided to develop border regions of the country through tourism. In a rural, impoverished region like Yunnan, where many other development projects had been tried and failed,[4] tourism seemed a sensible way to generate quick cash flows, especially of foreign currency, with relatively low requirements of capital investment and training. Economic development, and with it infrastructure improvements, would implicitly also facilitate state control of the often unstable borderlands.

By the late 1980s Yunnan had already become a beacon for foreign backpackers toting the Lonely Planet. But as it turned out, many of Yunnan's areas, including Sipsongpanna, were not suitable for the expansion to the mass tourist destinations that the state planners had in mind: they lacked adequate roads, electricity, and phone lines. Thus, China turned to international investors. Regional conferences on the "Golden Quadrangle"—the border areas of Yunnan, Laos, Burma, and Thailand—invoked visions of wealthy Southeast Asian entrepreneurs pouring up the Mekong into China and spoke of an "Asian growth zone" building on the then-popular "Asian values."[5]

However, as things happened Thailand crashed and China boomed, and domestic tourism became the surprise success story in Yunnan. Foreign visits to Yunnan increased by only three million between 1985 and 1992 but domestic visits leapt by ninety million. Three- and four-star hotels replaced the rough-and-ready stilt-house hostels run by ethnic minorities to serve foreign backpackers. Entrepreneurs who had prospered in new Special Economic Zones, such as Shenzhen, came to Yunnan with capital and service-sector experience and built larger businesses than had ever been seen in the region before, ones that could not for the most part be supplied by local producers.

Meanwhile, local governments in Yunnan began scrambling to compete for Chinese and transnational investment. Infrastructure improvements were the easiest to procure funding for, and so local governments destroyed and rebuilt Yunnan's sewers and roads multiple times, no doubt profiting from both construction contracts and building permit fees. Any unusual tree could be turned into a tourist destination for city dwellers who could not tell one palm tree from the next. Call it the "king of big leaves tree park," train some village girls to sway seductively in ethnic garb to recorded music, and charge for tickets at the gate. All such tourist destinations could

be the hubs from which sprung restaurants, karaoke lounges, brothels, and gambling halls—and these, in turn, required more roads
and electricity. Tourism fever swept Yunnan.

In Jinghong, Manting Road became the focal point for tourist
development. Every successful tourist town in the world probably
has a place like it: a humming, hybrid pedestrian street lined with
hotels, brothels, cafés, dance halls, and dangling street signs. On
a warm Friday night, anyone sitting in a Manting Road café could
watch a parade of barbecue sellers, grimy-faced, begging children
in Akha ethnic costume, bicyclers carrying live squawking chickens,
clusters of shouting Sichuanese tourists in matching baseball caps
and high-waisted pants, and Tai Lüe women strolling to and from
the market with baskets of fruit. A pair of men taking their sons
home from school bike together slowly, chatting, while the two little
boys, each perched on the back of his father's bike, talk with similar animation, hands flying. Chinese and Thai tourists, fresh after a
short flight from Kunming, ride high in their tour buses and peer
down in astonishment at bearded Dutch or Japanese tourists, dishev-
eled from thirty hours on a public bus. The foreigners lurch under
the improbable weight of their towering backpacks, guidebooks in
hand, in search of a café selling cold local beer. To many of these
visitors, Manting Road was home base, a place that brought together
the pleasantly strange with the comfortingly familiar. Some foreign
travelers lingered on Manting Road for weeks or months, sipping
the local Lancang beers and swapping travel tips with café-owners. It
was foreign backpackers like these, taking arduous bus rides down
from Kunming in the 1980s and early 1990s, who had put Sipsongpanna on the tourist map in the first place.

Dean MacCannell calls such displays the "front stage" of the tourism industry.[6] In order to attract tourists to this region, local and national governments had to reinvent the previously unstable borderlands
and make them a space of play. Traveling down Manting Road, visitors
could see theme parks that turned local ethnic peoples into objects of
visual pleasure. They could see dance shows set to new Chinese pop
tunes in ethnic-themed restaurants; these shows extended the objecti-
fication of ethnic bodies for the male consumer. At night, they could
stop into Manting Road brothels or visit underground casinos in hotels

for a taste of illicit pleasure. The tourist performances helped to turn all of Sipsongpanna into a theme park, a safe place where tourists could come for relaxation, consumption, and an encounter with exoticism.

The Ethnic Theme Park

> [The ethnic theme park] let you go into such land of primitive and crude, full of blood and enjoyment, containing signs and excitement of human history. . . . Please, stay here longer. Here are various national dances and you will can't help drinking yourself down there [sic]!
> —Xishuangbanna Nationalities Theme Park brochure

JINGHONG'S NATIONALITIES THEME PARK ("Minzu fengqing yuan"), built by the prefectural government in the mid-1990s, is Jinghong's most popular tourist attraction and the first stop for most visitors. I visited it soon after arriving. The theme park immerses visitors in a clean, ordered world of bounded ethnic groups, a model community that metonymically stands for the actual border region beyond its gates. The theme park presents a series of discrete ethnic groups living happily under the shadow of a towering monument that symbolizes the nation-state. These ethnic peoples, posing in costume in "in-situ" village settings, are presented as objects to be consumed and collected, not unlike the souvenirs that are also sold from their "ethnic houses." Such theme parks are scattered around China; they are enormously popular as attractions and play an important role in the discursive production of China's borders.

Jinghong's park is typical of other theme parks in China, such as the Kunming Nationalities Villages or the Shenzhen Splendid China Park: it presents these groups as childlike, miniaturized; primitive, but in ways that, like the naïveté and wildness of children, are safe and appealing to spectators.[7] Minorities who themselves perform in the park are represented not as thinking subjects but as aesthetic objects to be gazed on (they rarely speak but when they do it is always in Chinese) and as authenticating presences for the in-situ displays. Many of their identifying attributes used here draw from the ethnic characteristics identified in 1950s ethnography and evoke premodern views of the imperial south.

6 *Monument commemorating the region's liberation by the People's Republic of China in the Xishuangbanna Nationalities Theme Park.*

Passing through the turnstile at the main gate of the park, the visitor first sees a tall four-sided monolith crowned with a Tai Lüe–style roof (fig. 6). This monolith writes the ethnic theme park, and the borders the theme park sits on, into the national "imagined community" in ways oddly like Anderson's description of tombs of Unknown Soldiers: "void as these tombs are of identifiable remains or immortal souls, they are nonetheless saturated with ghostly *national* imaginings."[8] In Chinese and Tai Lüe script on alternate faces, the monument memorializes China's "liberation" of Sipsongpanna and implicitly asserts the role of the theme park in the official discourse about ethnic identity within the nation-state.

Passing the monolith, visitors meander down cobblestoned paths, past forests of trees planted with perfect symmetry—a statement both about the lush nature for which Sipsongpanna is famous and about the need for humans to discipline nature. The paths lead past concrete arenas that feature scheduled Tai Lüe "peacock dances" and live elephant shows. One path winds past a small animal zoo and then finishes in a series of Tai Lüe, Akha, and Lahu ethnic "villages." These villages are small, bounded clusters of miniature stilt houses. Women in ethnic costumes lounge around some of the houses, chatting with visitors, urging them to buy refreshments or souvenirs, and posing for photographs on request. The miniaturization of ethnic homes reduces ethnic peoples to the stature of children, enhancing the status of the visitor.

In her discussion of the Splendid China Park in Shenzhen, Ann Anagnost notes regarding a miniaturized replica of the Tibetan Potala Palace that "a powerfully divisive force is here domesticated and rendered purely as display."[9] These displays are ahistorical; ethnic minorities in the theme park are presented as they were, supposedly, before liberation—in a state of nature. Each village in the theme

7 *Miniature Tai Lüe houses in the theme park also serve as gift shops.*

8 *Inmates manufacturing ethnic batiks at a forced detoxification center near Kunming.*
PHOTO COURTESY OF HUMAN RIGHTS WATCH.

park is identical in format—a cluster of small stilt houses off the main path. Thus the layout of the theme park creates expectations of similarity and of seriality, minimizing the complexity of ethnic difference but underscoring the collectibility and commodification of ethnic encounters.[10] In these cheerful performances for visiting tourists, complexities of history and nuances of local culture are discarded in favor of repetitive and similar presentations of ethnic costume, song, dance, and souvenirs.

Some of the village stilt houses literally commodify ethnicity—they also function as gift shops selling souvenirs: shoulder bags, jade jewelry, and batik textiles (fig. 7). The presence of these ethnic objects adds an authenticating flair; however, they are not locally made. According to one souvenir shop owner in the theme park, the souvenirs are manufactured in factories in southeast China and shipped to the theme park for sale. A visit I made much later to a prison outside of Kunming where injection drug users are detained revealed unpaid inmates mass-manufacturing similar batiks and fake jade (fig. 8).[11]

Drawing on Jane Desmond's work, we could call the Xishuang-banna theme park villages an "in-fake-situ" display: like a map, the ethnic theme park re-stages on a smaller scale the world that sur-rounds the park itself.[12] The "physical evidence" of the living bodies of people in ethnic dress authenticates the villages and the souve-nirs around them.

But, like any map, the theme park is carefully edited. There are no references, for instance, to ethnic participation in contemporary media, business, education, or other industries. Ethnic minorities are situated in the past; theme parks stress their categorization as "backward, primitive." There are also no references here to the rela-tionship of any of Sipsongpanna's minority groups with ethnically related groups across the borders, literally a few hours away. The national border is drawn sharply here. Not all bodies from Sip-songpanna are given equal time: Hans, for instance, who make up one third of the population of the prefecture, do not have a village display in the theme park. Despite the fascination of many Chi-nese tourists with foreign backpackers there is also no "barbarian village" on display. Hans and foreigners are the subjects who con-sume the displays, not the objects; they are the "ideal spectators" for whom the display is designed.[13] Like nineteenth-century U.K. and U.S. museum displays of living African, North American, and even Asian peoples, which showed them engaged in cooking, nursing, and acting out "the drama of the quotidian,"[14] the Xishuangbanna theme park uses living people in in-fake-situ displays to people the borders in the imaginations of the dominators.

Elsewhere, Louisa Schein and Dru Gladney have both called the exoticized representations of minorities in Chinese mass media as "internal Orientalism."[15] Gladney suggests that these domestic rep-resentations of ethnic Others discursively produce a sophisticated, modern, Han self. But these images, including living displays like the theme parks, actually create a national whole. The ways in which these state-sanctioned public representations of minorities infantilize, simplify, and exoticize them emphasize the belief that minorities are on the lowest rung in China's social-evolutionary ladder—a low point that happens to coincide with the geographical borders. To go lower in social organization than the Wa or Lahu is to risk falling off the map of the world—*this way monsters lie.*

In addition, theme parks and other mass media representations of ethnic minorities in China, when combined with the repressive apparatus of the state, instruct minorities in the allowable limits of public ethnic identity. The message to ethnic groups is carrot and stick: Enrich yourself through self-commodification, or express other kinds of ethnic identity and create trouble for yourself with the police.

* * *

AFTER VISITING THE theme park, most tourists in Sipsongpanna also went to ethnic-themed restaurants along Manting Road to watch dance shows. Similar restaurants and ethnic dance revues have now become popular in many Chinese cities.

Minority-Themed Restaurants

IN THE PURSUIT of knowledge, I ate dinners and watched dance revues at approximately a dozen "minority-themed," "Dai-flavor," and "minority-atmosphere" restaurants along both sides of Manting Road.[16] The dances in these revues vary little from the dance shows performed in ethnic theme parks or at international performances by government song-and-dance troupes. In some cases, choreographers and dancers for those troupes do freelance work at the restaurants. The restaurant shows tend to heighten the sexuality in the dance revues, turning them into highly gendered displays for mostly male audiences.

To ensure that I got a table at these restaurants, which often turn away individual diners, I hired my new friend Rebecca, known to her friends as Bex. Bex was a Welsh backpacker who had come to

Sipsongpanna to teach English. Along with several other English teachers she had been ejected from the local teacher training college when it was discovered that some (not including Bex) were Christian missionaries. She moved off campus and stayed in town, tutoring on the side, and we met in a Manting Road backpacker café called Journey to the East.

Bex had a no-nonsense grunge style; she sported a nose ring and had shaved her head because, she said, hair was "too hot to bother with" in Jinghong's subtropical heat. Though the only other people most Jinghong residents had ever seen with shaved heads were Buddhist monks, and though her appearance often drew stares and comments (the most common being "*Wah, wo yiwei ni shi nande,*" or "Whoah, I thought you were a man"), Bex always shrugged it off. The jokes always turned to frank expressions of admiration of her individualism and, inevitably, toasts of rice liquor that lasted well into the evening. All of this qualified Bex for a position as research assistant in a project that mostly involved eating and drinking. Having clarified that my research grant would pay for dinner, she pronounced herself ready to get to work.

The work turned out to be more arduous than it seemed—the dance revues soon acquired a numbing sameness. Within a few days of beginning our research we were in danger of losing track of which restaurants we had been to and which we had not. All the restaurants, many of which were built in stilt houses that had been Tai Lüe homes, opened their front gates at six-thirty. All of them had similar signs in front. At 6:45, all of them simultaneously filled Manting Road with the sound of cymbals and gongs as young women in identical polyester versions of Tai Lüe costume emerged. They leaned on the restaurants' wooden gates and splashed the guests with water from silver bowls, mimicking the famous Tai Lüe new year festival. Buses arrived, groups of Chinese tourists in matching baseball caps filed off behind tour guides waving little flags, and the young women sullenly sprinkled everyone with water. Bex and I filed in behind the crowd to look for seats, arguing based on the decor whether we had been in this restaurant before or not.

The decor, unfortunately, often provided no clue. Inside each dining hall the walls and ceilings were decorated with plastic vines and tree boughs and, in some cases, red velour stage curtains. The floor was filled with round tables and folding chairs and the tour groups crammed around them. On each table were versions of Tai Lüe food—including the famous sticky rice, fried ferns, barbecued beef, and pineapple stuffed with sweet rice, but omitting such Tai Lüe staples as roaring hot chili sauce, liquified raw beef, pig entrails, bamboo grubs, and deep-fried buffalo rinds. Once the guests were seated the rice liquor began to flow, and each restaurant filled with the loud sounds of toasts as similar cheers echoed down Manting Road from neighboring restaurants.

Soon after, the dance revues began, introduced by a male emcee shouting into a microphone. The emcee urged visiting groups to identify themselves and cheer for their hometowns. Restaurant dance troupes, containing mostly women, then came out on a platform stage to do a series of Tai, Akha, Bulang, Lahu, Yao, and other ethnic dances. For each dance the same group of dancers performed, only switching costumes to indicate a different ethnicity. It did not matter which ethnicity the dancers were—in fact, most of them were Hans. Tai Lües in Jinghong said that only one of the Manting Road restaurants was owned by and hired Tai Lües (though they did not agree which restaurant that was). None were said to be owned by members of other ethnic groups.

Each of the restaurant revues included many of the same dance routines as we saw at the others—the routines were borrowed from the state song-and-dance troupes. Invariably, an introductory dance showed various ethnic minorities tilling fields, bathing in rivers, washing bowls, and donning sarongs with stylized movements, accompanied by smiles aimed at the male audience. A Tai Lüe dance usually had women in long skirts swaying their hips back and forth onstage while posing with silver bowls and smiling provocatively; this number ended with the women filling their bowls with water and splashing surprised audience members. Another, the peacock dance, featured a woman wearing a skirt decorated to look like it was made of peacock feathers spinning in ballet shoes (this dance is discussed more in a later chapter). At the end of these shows, in a play on the long-defunct Tai Lüe courting ritual, women twirled little cotton pouches on strings while bobbing their hips and then

9 *Women in Tai Lüe costume perform a courtship dance for tourists.*

tossed the pouches at their "suitors," the predominantly male and predominantly drunken audience (fig. 9). In one show, the emcee chose an audience member to be crowned as the Tai Lüe king and allowed him to pick a dancer as his queen.

The final element that reinforced the strange sameness of these shows was musical: all the restaurants on Manting Road staged their revues to the same cassette, a collection of Chinese-language pop songs about minorities titled *Xishuangbanna fengqing* (Xishuangbanna atmosphere).[17] This fusion of ethnic exoticism and instrumentation with Chinese lyrics and musical styles created a genre of pop music aimed at Hans—"touropop." One especially popular song on this tape was "Xishuangbanna, wode jiaxiang" (Xishuangbanna, my hometown).[18] The singer's voice, claiming the hometown for herself and her visiting listeners, played from speakers in dozens of cafés on the streets of Jinghong all day, as well as from the main gates of the ethnic theme park. By night, the song echoed up and down Manting Road, with a clamor of gongs, strings, and flutes:

Beat the drum! Strike the gong!
Sing a song of our loveable home!
Rolling hills covered with gold,
An ocean of green rubber tree forests,
Melons and fruits sweet all year long,
And our justly famous fragrant tea!
Ah! Ah! Ah! Ah!
The ancient forests are a treasure trove!
An elephant bows his head in blessing!
Lala, lala, lala, la-la—
Xishuangbanna—my hometown!

Beat the drum! Strike the gong!
Sing a song of our loveable home!
The Lancang [Mekong] River weaves rosy clouds of dawn,
The evening bell of a Burmese temple fills the moonlight,
Young men stand straight as rows of palm trees,
And young girls smell sweeter than the exotic Burmese flowers!
Ah! AH! AH! AH!
Mystical place, mystical wind!
The peacock lifts his wings above the clouds!
Ah! Ah! AH! AH!
XI-SHUANG-BAN-NAAAAA
MY HOOOME TOOOOWWWN

Painting Sipsongpanna's landscape and ethnic cultures in vivid
Technicolor, this touropop song builds an image of a wondrous land,
a "treasure trove" of collectible objects: hills, rubber trees, melons,
fruits, tea, rivers, temples, peacocks, and, of course, young girls. The
song gives a litany of objects that the theme park brings to life.

Note that in this orgiastic recitation of exotic objects and delights,
we are once again being given a map. This hybrid song puts a series
of collectible exotic objects in a frame that makes them familiar. The
singer is herself Tai Lüe, but she sings in Chinese. A second verse,
sung in Tai Lüe and probably intended to give an air of authenticity,
was said by one Tai Lüe listener to be so grammatically incorrect
that it made no sense. The music is martial and musically Han Chi-

nese (in terms of its tonality and melody), performed by a collection of Yunnanese ethnic instruments that have probably never been played together at any other moment in history.

COLLECTIVELY, THE THEME PARK with its lounging women in ethnic dress, the touropop songs, and the dances performed to them by sinuous women, all draw on long-standing Chinese ideas about southern peoples. The images of ethnic women here—the flirtatious dancing girls, the happy singers, and the flower-like girls—also evoke imagery and poetry created by the Tang Empire about the women of the south. Edward Schafer describes Han and Tang conquests of modern-day Guangdong and northern Vietnam as creating a tradition in Chinese culture in which the south is "the land of seductive women and attractive landscapes."[19] Tang and Song poets eulogized the laugh of the southern enchantress, the "wickedly enticing" girl framed by banana groves, painted boats, and clouds of brilliant flowers.[20] Some southern women were also viewed as dangerous: Norma Diamond charts the historical rise, over centuries, of Chinese legends linking Miao (Hmong) temptresses to poison, another image that arose from the empire's southern expansion.[21] These premodern representations now attract capital to the borderlands: tourist brochures produced by the prefectural government featured photographs of Tai women smiling coyly at the camera from under parasols (fig. 10). A brochure produced by the Tai Garden Hotel, Jinghong's five-star hotel, presented photographs of naked women bathing in rivers in which the women appeared to be angry, covering themselves up and fleeing from the photographer. According to tour guides in Jinghong and foreign scholars, tour buses often trawled the back roads in search of Tai Lüe women who could be photographed while bathing in the Mekong River.[22]

These images are also a way for Tai Lües to manage their relationship with the central state. In some respects, they evoke the tributary performances with which ethnic kingdoms welcomed Chinese imperial emissaries in the past. Imperial China developed an elaborate, ritualized system of tributary exchanges to cement relationships with smaller neighboring states in Central Asia and Southeast Asia. Chinese tributary delegations regularly journeyed to imperial outposts for

傣家女
Dai girls

西雙版納傣族自治州人民政府
The Government of Xishuangbanna
Dai Autonomous Prefecture

10 *A prefectural government brochure markets the images of Tai Lüe women.*

ritualized orchestral music performances. In return, the smaller states developed their own orchestras to perform for the visiting imperial delegations. Imperial delegates then presented the local states with Chinese goods and in return received goods that brought a steady flow of new arts, music, wealth, and sometimes people (artisans, dancing women, oral poets) into imperial capitals. Through these transnational ritual exchanges, many objects and people traveled across tens of thousands of miles. Some musical instruments moved from the Central Asian deserts east to the imperial capital where they became Chinese classical instruments, then were in turn passed south to Thailand and Burma, even as far as to the islands of the Pacific.

The flows of goods and skills into China from beyond its borders enriched Chinese empires, but the tributary exchange had advantages to the smaller states as well. By ceding face to the imperial visitors, offering warm hospitality, presenting a few souvenir trinkets, and sending out the local girls to smile and dance, a tiny state in rural Southeast Asia could manage the empire's intrusion into its region while continuing largely to govern itself. The shadow of the tributary exchange system stands behind contemporary tourism; Sipsongpanna Tai Lües still dance for the empire while trying to hold it at bay. And some of those Tai Lües found ways to directly profit from the influx of wealthy imperialists and their fascination with southern "temptresses."

The Underworld

MOST NIGHTS, AFTER dinner and a show, crowds of male Chinese tourists spilled out into Manting Road. They were greeted there by hundreds of women, most of whom were Han Chinese migrants from other provinces, wearing Tai Lüe skirts to attract tourists who had heard that ethnic women were sexually "open." Along Manting Road, in the spaces between the official shows and the foreign cafés were darker shadows—the illegal businesses that formed the foundation of the local economy.

Some performers in dance halls finished dance revues by offering free massages and sex for pay. Hundreds more women sat in the dimmed red light of storefront karaoke lounges and barbershops or rode around the central park in bicycle trishaws, waiting for men in trishaws to hail them. Sipsongpanna was so famous for its sex trade that some tourists admitted they had lied to their wives about where they were going over the weekend. Because of the paucity of information about HIV/AIDS in China, many people probably did not know how the virus was transmitted or how to prevent it.

Besides the sex trade, other kinds of illicit economies sprouted up in Jinghong. Hotel casinos were raided and closed with great fanfare when a delegation of high-ranking officials came to town, only to reopen a few days after they left. Shipments of alcohol, drugs, gemstones, and weapons traveling up the Mekong River were sometimes seized and displayed on local television, but the occasional crackdowns never really interfered with business that profited local authorities. Jinghong's streets were lined with Japanese cars and trucks smuggled in from Thailand, many belonging to government officials. Some of Manting Road's newest and most elaborate houses were rumored to belong to famous Golden Triangle drug dealers.

Between the illegal market and the official tourist front stage, the backpacker cafés on Manting Road sat uneasily. These cafés are now a globalizing phenomenon. They are alternate spaces, lying simultaneously inside and outside of the country in which they are situated, and they have a remarkable sameness from Kathmandu to Koh Samui. Some Jinghong locals viewed the backpacker cafés as vice-ridden places that were best avoided. At the same time, the cafés could be prestigious places to be seen, because all things foreign were cool through their association with wealth and modernity. Though they scrimped and bargained religiously, the backpackers formed a cutting-edge elite in Sipsongpanna. In the 1980s and 1990s they had "discovered" Jinghong and in some ways sparked all the tourist development that followed. For some of the local women, a male backpacker could be a ticket out of poverty to wealth and comfort. The cafés were also the first spaces in which I heard inklings of ethnic critiques of the tourist displays.

On my initial visit to Manting Road that first night in Jinghong, I found myself at Journey to the East, a local institution. Its manager was a young woman, Anulan, who simultaneously supervised the kitchen and the love lives of her customers with dry wit and generosity. By day, when the foreign backpackers climbed on their rented bikes and wobbled off in search of authentic ethnic encounters, ethnic minorities from Jinghong poured into Journey to the East.

These customers were Anulan's peers, young people born in local villages who were drawn to Jinghong as a town where they could make a freer life away from the watchful gaze of village elders. Ironically, some Chinese tourists had been drawn to Sipsongpanna because they imagined this conservative rural region to be a free zone of sexual and cultural experimentation. Instead, the presence of all these visitors with money and status was producing wild women or attracting them from other places. Some of the women who danced in ethnic costume by night came to Journey to the East and the local discos dressed in miniskirts and jeans, looking for foreign friends, especially foreign boyfriends. Jinghong was full of Cinderella stories: local women who had caught the eye of passing travelers and had won a lottery ticket—a free ride to lives of comfort in Tokyo, Texas, or Seoul—or so the fairy tale went.

Some of the Jinghong women I got to know were banking on this fairy tale. E La, a Tai Lüe woman of my age, told me that she would never marry a Jinghong man because they "lie and cheat" and beat their wives. She had made a foreign marriage part of her life plan. In Jinghong, because the exoticism of ethnic women to Chinese and foreign men made it easier to marry up, *"nüren shi laoda, nanren shi laoer,"* she joked: women are top dog and men are number two. Outside of the marriage lottery, Jinghong women faced a limited array of employment options: farmer, hotel maid, desk clerk, waitress, tour guide, dancer.

The women at Journey to the East were joined by Jinghong's handful of semi-openly gay and bisexual men, some of whom also worked as dancers. Onstage, they cavorted as happy savages for the Han crowds; offstage, they were Jinghong's fashionable epitome of urban sophistication and wit. Through Anulan, I became friendly with a sweet-natured young man from a prominent local Han family, one of the few who openly said he was bisexual. One day we ran into each other on the bus from Gasa (in Tai, Gatsai), a neighboring town, and I asked casually how he was. "I don't know," he answered seriously. "I know I should be upbeat [*kaixin*] and I want to be upbeat, but I can't get myself into a good mood. I know my family loves me, but somehow I always have a feeling of pressure in my heart."

All the sex on Manting Road had helped fuel the tourism boom in Sipsongpanna. But as the state was willing to turn a blind eye to the sex trade in Jinghong, it also covered up the violence that sometimes attached to it. In the mid-1990s, a half-Swiss, half-Brazilian backpacker who lived on Manting Road for a few months was detained in connection with the rape and murder of a teenage Tai Lüe girl whose body was found on the banks of the Mekong River. After a long detention the man was deported. The girl's family was reported to have accepted a payment of the equivalent of a few thousand U.S. dollars for dropping the charges. The local newspapers never reported the murder, and a Swiss journalist who investigated the case told us that local police would not discuss it.

Over a dinner of snails, fried rice, and beer in 2001, in a wooden stilt-house restaurant overlooking a sunset across rice fields, Tai Lüe friends brought up the incident again and spoke with some bitterness over the way it had been handled. "China wants to join the World Trade Organization," said one Tai Lüe man. "They want to do business with the West. How can one Tai girl's life compare to that?" Other dinner guests were grim and quiet. Someone else hushed up the controversial conversation by proposing a toast to international friendship. Four years after the murder, these local residents spoke about it as if it were yesterday. It stood for the many small injustices that had occurred in the intervening years, all the smaller stories of violence, corruption, and abuse that whittled away at the fifty-year-old promise of ethnic autonomy. But these diners were just as scathing about what greed had done to indigenous social relationships and about the Tai Lüe family that they said had sold their daughter's life cheaply. "We Tai people feel that this was not right," said the first speaker again, slowly and in Mandarin to make sure that I understood.

Tourism development in Sipsongpanna had used the images of dancing women to domesticate the borderlands. The industry flourished because of the sex trade, the drug trade, and the gambling that went on in the spaces between theme park displays. Tourism had also opened up spaces for experimentation with new and alternative ways of living. But even some of the foreign backpackers who had inadvertently helped to fuel the development of tourism took a dim view. At Journey to the East I got to know Mat, a sunburned, tough, Welsh retiree who was backpacking around the world and who had settled in a shabby hotel on Manting Road, living next door to dishwashers, cab drivers, and sex workers.

Mat ate all his meals at Journey to the East but he did not approve of Chinese-style mass tourism. One day soon after I arrived he sat by the window of the café and pointed his arm out the window at a building across the street with wordless disgust. Groups of construction workers, bare to the waist, were standing on beams and swinging hammers to smash the concrete walls and ceilings around them. The sound of hammers echoed down the street. Mat slapped the table. "Ridiculous," he said. "Now they're building a parking lot. Five years ago it was a pond that the whole town fished in; then a perfectly pleasant little park; then a set of useful shops; now they're turning it into a parking lot for tour buses. Why don't they build something local people can use?" He stubbed the table with his forefinger. "Tomfoolery! This government is in a fever, and when it passes all of this is going to be a god-awful mess. They're wrecking the town, mark my words, and when it's done they're going to wish they'd asked me, but it'll be too late." He leaned back and began industriously to pick his teeth. "I'll have moved on."

Anulan came in to clear away his soup bowl. "You and Bex go see dancing tonight?" she asked me, practicing her English.

I said that we would and asked if she had seen any of these song-and-dance shows. Anulan rolled her eyes and switched back to Chinese. "Why would I go? That stuff is boring."

"The locals don't recognize themselves in that stuff," said Mat.

"Those dancers are all a bunch of *saobi*," said Anulan, laughing, using a crass Chinese slang term for promiscuous women.

While they lived in them, created them, and profited from them, many locals had nothing but ironic disgust for the businesses that lined Manting Road. And this was expressed in one curious way: no one in Jinghong except tourists, who learned its name from the map produced for them, accepted that Manting Road existed. Getting into a trishaw anywhere in Jinghong and asking the driver to take me to Manting Road, the town's most popular and bustling street, invariably resulted only in a shrug and a confused expression. Anulan explained: "You have to tell him to bring you to Ban Tin," the name of the Tai Lüe village that had once occupied the area. Locals were keeping a vanished geography alive—a whole other kind of imagined community.

While profiting local entrepreneurs and their friends in local government and obscuring its reliance on an underground economy in sex and drugs, the officially sanctioned and commodified representations of ethnic minority identity in turn endorsed and undergirded paternalistic central state policies. They had helped to incorporate Sipsongpanna more fully into the Chinese nation. But my own search for ethnic authenticity, which inevitably mirrored that of foreign backpackers, led past Ban Tin and over the end of Manting Road into a trans-border Tai-speaking world that organized itself around a different geography.

Backstage

ON THE OFFICIAL tourist map, Manting Road winds down to a curve around Chunhuan Park, where the page abruptly stops. On a weekday morning, a bicyclist cruising down the last slope of the hill passed the end of the commercial stretch and, as it were, bicycled off the edge of the page and into a quiet residential area. Here were a few majestic trees, an elementary school, a barbershop, and a market with vegetables laid out on tarps on the road. In 1997 and 1998, this was a sunny and peaceful street. At the main entrance to Chunhuan Park the street turned quietly into a path running through a network of Tai Lüe villages and fields that ultimately led to the next major town, Gatsai.

There was no marker of what had been here before, but this part of Jinghong had a long history as the capital of Sipsongpanna. The region's largest Buddhist temple was hidden far in back of Chunhuan Park on the top of a hill. In the past, the city-state known as Muang Jinghong had ruled an alliance of twelve townships, each ruled by a noble family. Jinghong's ruling prince lived in a palace, the royal forest of which is now Chunhuan Park. The temple, Wat Pajay, was the head temple for the region, and its abbot advised the prince. According to local oral legend, it was built on ground chosen by the Buddha himself. Chinese imperial officials, meanwhile, occupied a barrack in a remote part of town now housing the prefectural government.

The path to Gatsai continued on to link Jinghong to other Tai-speaking city-states along the Mekong Delta, which historically allied with each other, fought with each other, brokered politically motivated marriages between their princes and princesses, and whose people traveled back and forth to celebrate the same major holidays. The written histories of these states make numerous references to their neighbors.[23] They also shared some of the same oral and literary canon.[24]

None of this is marked in any way at Chunhuan Park—all that history is invisible to the visitor. Chunhuan Park is another small, pleasant, ethnic theme park. Buying a ticket at the entry gate, the visitor walks along a stone path to a stage where performers in Tai Lüe costume sing and dance for tourists. The path goes by an elephant that is chained to a tree and poses for photographs, a peacock petting zoo, and a stand where the visitor can dress up as Tai Lüe royalty and pose for photographs in front of what looks like a Buddhist reliquary. Finally the path, crossing a river, reaches the *Zong Fosi* ("Central Buddhist temple"), or, in Tai Lüe, *Wat Pajay*. The prefectural government had helped to build the main hall and dormitory of the current structure when it constructed Chunhuan Park in 1990. In 1997 and 1998 Wat Pajay housed the thirty-eight-year-old abbot and eighty-five monks and novices, ranging in age from twelve to forty.[25] Tourists who make it this far into the theme park often stroll the grounds of the temple, coming into the main hall to bow to the images of the Buddha that were donated from Thailand.

Wat Pajay has a twin existence in both of Jinghong's two geographies, however: while it stands in the back of the theme park and off the official map of Jinghong, it also stands on a hill over which paths run down to a network of Tai Lüe villages across the unmapped valley. On holidays, Tai Lüe villagers stream up this hill, carrying gifts, food, and blankets, and take over the temple grounds, speaking a

different language, preparing a different kind of food, bowing to
the young monks, and making offerings. Their conversations with
the monks and the monks' conversations with one other often contested the public representations of Tais for tourists. Most of the
temple's senior monks and lay supporters saw Tai Lüe culture as
threatened by assimilation pressures and by the state's lack of support for indigenous ethnic expression. They saw the temple as the
best hope for both social and cultural strengthening of Tai Lües. A
common refrain I heard on the grounds of the temple was, "No one
cares about our Tai culture—only the temple cares."

The temple serves as the head school for novice monks, teaching
novices Tai Lüe language, history, culture, and religious practice.
In ways similar to other Theravada Buddhist temples in Southeast
Asia, Wat Pajay also functions as a community center. Moreover, the
rebuilding and revival of Wat Pajay has permitted Chinese Tai Lüe
monks to travel across the borders to study in Thai temples. In a
kind of civilizing project from the opposite vector, some Thai monks
see donations and assistance to Wat Pajay as meritorious charity, reviving a lost Buddhist tradition. As the next chapter will show, these
cross-border flows have brought new technological skills, new values, and new ideas that will reshape Sipsongpanna in the future.

Conclusions

AS A VISITOR to the Chinese borders sets out of the hotel, guidebook
in hand, ready to seek new experiences that she has seen and imagined first in text, she walks along ruts in the ground formed by
centuries of economic and political forces. The geography created
by maps, theme parks, dances, and songs created for tourists draws
on centuries of imperial Chinese tropes about southwestern border
peoples, the recent government "ethnic identification" projects, and
the forces of capital driving the sex trade and other underground
economies. Together, these forces create a front-stage sphere that
shapes ethnic identity representations allowed within the context of
the Chinese nation-state.

At the same time, the unleashing of market forces on these borders created new openings, interstitial and fluid spaces of dissent,

illicit economies, and ethnic and religious activism. Behind the scenes of the tourist display, locals were involved in reviving and reinventing the region's history, critiquing the state's consecration of ethnic identity, and moving through openings on the borders to seek new and old ideas.

2

Song and Silence

I t was time to get to work. A few mornings after my arrival, with courage drunk from a few cups of strong coffee at Journey to the East, I crammed into a phone booth at the Xishuangbanna Binguan and struggled to shut the glass doors—a symbolic exercise, as the phone booth lacked a ceiling. Nothing could be done without monitoring. A hotel guest wishing to make a telephone call had to come to the business center, give the number to a young woman in a navy suit with a white neck ruffle, and wait while she noted the number in a register and dialed it. The clerk's eyes widened when I handed her the phone number I wished to call: it belonged to Mr. Dao, a senior local-government official, the Tai Lüe friend of a Chinese friend.[1] The woman with the neck ruffle sat down to watch and listen. On the phone, Mr. Dao urged me to come to his office, "Right now!"

I had come to Sipsongpanna to conduct doctoral research for one year into the subject of Tai Lüe oral poetry, but the truth was that no one knew if there was anything left to study. The few Chinese books on Tai Lües in U.S. libraries made no mention of it. I had only two leads. First, Heather Peters, an archaeologist who had worked in Sipsongpanna in the 1980s, said she had once seen a female oral poet perform in a temple, chanting while holding a fan in front of her face. Second, I had found a Chinese graduate thesis in the library, published in India, with a brief reference to Tai Lüe oral poets as healers.[2] The smooth talking that had gotten me a grant for this tenuous project couldn't carry it any further: now I had to get the goods, which meant getting behind the front stage, if possible. In this early phase I began to become aware of an expanding backstage sphere, an arena of written and sung culture that Tai Lües performed not for others but for themselves. In the beginning, some apparently open doors closed quickly, while other doors that seemed closed turned out to lead to places that could not have been foreseen. Moving from front stage to backstage required crossing social boundaries that had been managed carefully for years.

The woman with the neck ruffle said that the prefectural government compound was across the street and around the corner, past the rows of stores in concrete boxes selling liquor and cigarettes, pop-music cassettes, and photocopies, and past the symmetrical lines of palm trees and the overlapping rings of bicycle bells. I arrived at a small, tree-filled compound guarded by a soldier in green on a pedestal. He stood ramrod straight with a rifle, staring impassively at the tops of the buildings across the street. Crowds of people appeared to be strolling nonchalantly in and out of the gateway below him, wheeling bicycles and leading children. I followed them and heard a shout. A woman tapped on my arm and pointed. The guard was shouting. I walked up to him. He shook his head while staring fiercely over my head at the horizon.

"I'm going to see Mr. Dao," I told him in Chinese. He shook his head again, still without lowering his gaze. Foreigners were strictly forbidden in a Chinese government compound—we could be spies. I had to go across the street to a store that rented its phone out for a few pennies and ask Mr. Dao to come out.

Short, broad-shouldered, and with a shock of black hair, Mr. Dao was a man with barely suppressed energy. He led the way through the pleasant, leafy compound, up a dirty old stairwell, and into his spacious and sunny office, where he gave me a hot glass of the famous local green tea. There was nothing on his desk except the day's newspaper and an ashtray. "He'll be much too busy to help with something like this," I had worried to the Chinese professor who had referred me to Mr. Dao. The professor laughed: "People are busy when they are working to get to the position Mr. Dao has now," he said. "Once they get there, they aren't busy anymore."

I presented a letter of introduction from this professor, which Mr. Dao gravely read. Much of what he then said had to be pieced together later, because my Chinese language skills weren't strong yet, and Mr. Dao had a pungent local accent.

"Good, good," he said. "You (unclear) Tai Lüe. How can I help?"

"Well, I would like to meet oral poets and interview them and also record their poetry. Are there any poets?"

"(Something unclear)," he said. "(Long speech in Yunnanese about minority folklore)." With ceremony, he unlocked a glass bookshelf behind him and pulled out a fat volume of Tai Lüe folk songs translated into Chinese, the flyleaf of which he signed with a flourish. In the United States I had read a few similar volumes of Chinese minority poetry and was to read more: joyful paeans to the Chinese Communist Party and the fine harvest, children's songs and nursery rhymes, all translated into politically correct Chinese without reference to the original Tai Lüe idioms or contexts. I thanked him and accepted the book. It seemed he was one of the editors.

"(Something in Yunnanese suggesting offer of help.)"

"I would like to study the Tai Lüe language," I said. "Can you recommend a teacher?"

He hemmed and hawed a bit then went into a longish speech in Yunnanese about the poor state of local education, which I couldn't understand, but nodded at. "The best is to go to the Central Buddhist Temple in Chunhuan Park," he concluded. "They teach children Tai Lüe, but whatever you do, don't (unclear). Anything else?"

"Could you recommend someone who could introduce me to oral poets?" I asked.

"Ah," he said. He thought for a moment, then picked up the phone, dialed a number, and began yelling in Yunnanese. Much of what he said—in fact, much of what everyone in Jinghong said—was punctuated by the word "ga." "You (unclear), ga!" he shouted. "I'm going to (unclear), ga! You (unclear), ga! There you are, ga," he said to me, hanging up the phone.

"Thank you very much," I said, unsure what had happened. Mr. Dao stood up and walked to the door, and I followed him. Were we finished already? Was it time for me to go? We walked down the stairs, me hesitantly trying to follow, he politely encouraging me to go first. We reached the courtyard. He waved to a man squatting on his heels under a tree and smoking a cigarette, who leapt up and got into a black sedan with tinted windows parked on the grass. "Get in the car," he said.

"Where are we going?" I asked.

He stared, astonished. "We're going to meet the singer," he said. "Didn't you understand me?"

We swept off in the black sedan to a small storefront café where a few people were sitting around a round table chatting. When Mr. Dao rushed up to the café with his typical energy, all of the people around the table immediately stood up, folded their hands in front of their faces, and bowed, performing the *wai*, a traditional local greeting. One of them was a woman of about forty dressed in Tai Lüe costume, with her hair in a bun, a wealth of gold jewelry, and a radiant smile.

"This is E Guang,"[3] said Mr. Dao. "She's the most famous singer in the region. She'll tell you everything there is to know." To E Guang he said, "You tell her everything she wants to know about our Tai Lüe songs, ga!" E Guang smiled and dropped a curtsy. Mr. Dao told me to contact him with any other questions and swept off again in his car.

E Guang and her friends invited me to sit with them at the round lunch table, and she poured me a glass of green tea. This storefront was E Guang's Tai Lüe café, renowned for its barbecue. "Would you like to come back to interview me and record my singing?" E Guang asked. We agreed that I would return at six, and I went back to the guesthouse, after barely an hour of fieldwork, in a state of elation. After years of courses on fieldwork methodology, I had found a major informant right out of the gate. This field research thing was turning out to be relatively easy and straightforward.

That night I returned to E Guang's café laden with several kinds of video- and audio-recording equipment and joined her and a group of local folklorists and culture bureau officials over a formal Tai Lüe meal in a private room in her café. E Guang sang a few Tai Lüe songs, which I recorded. One of the officials accompanied her on the *bi*, a bamboo reed instrument that resembled a flute, and on the *erhu*, a two-stringed Chinese violin. The songs had lilting melodies; the lyrics, she said, praised the beauty of Sipsongpanna and welcomed an honored visitor from far away. I learned only later that these were the kind of formal odes Sipsongpanna oral poets normally perform for visiting officials from Beijing—tributary performances. While there was something a bit staged about the songs and the cheers and toasts of the guests, and though E Guang blushingly declined the payment I offered her in front of the others, overall the evening seemed to have gone pretty well.

✳ ✳ ✳

THE NEXT MORNING I followed Mr. Dao's second suggestion and bicycled out to the temple, passing Anulan and her sister, who were opening up the Journey to the East café for the day. At the main gate of Chunhuan Park I paid a fifteen-yuan entry fee and walked the bicycle back, over a hill and a bridge and past the brightly-painted Buddhist reliquaries, to Wat Pajay (fig. 11). The bald boy novices swinging on the main metal gate to the temple whispered to each other and smiled as I entered. I locked the bike where it stood, as a pickup truck full of seated monks, all staring, bounced by, then walked up the main steps, where a teenage monk was collecting donations and selling incense to people visiting the large golden

11 *Wat Pajay, the central Buddhist temple.*

image of the Buddha. "You want to study Tai Lüe language?" asked the monk with some surprise. A more senior monk of about forty was found; he invited me into a back room and offered me pomelo and tamarind from a fruit bowl on his table. Other monks came in and watched as the senior monk, a thin, dark man with an inward-looking gaze, mulled over the problem. "Right now we are preparing to observe the end of *Vasaa*," he said eventually, referring to the holiday that ends a summer retreat period. "Please come back next Tuesday."

In many of the older Buddhist stories a disciple is put through tests in order to prove his desire to attain enlightenment. I returned the Tuesday after Vasaa on the bicycle again, wearing the long skirt that friends at Journey to the East said was appropriate for the Buddhist temple. My arrival caused a small ruckus. A novice was sent to find the senior monk, and in their rooms the senior monks held a lengthy internal discussion about what to do with the foreign woman who wanted to study the Tai Lüe language.

With the reinstatement of some religious freedoms in China in 1989, Tai Lüe Buddhism had begun to flourish again. Kiyoshi Hasegawa reports that in the 1950s there were 574 temples in Sipsongpanna and 6,449 monks and novices.[4] After the Cultural Revolution, in 1981, this number was down to 145 temples and 655 novices. In 1997, Wat Pajay housed about seventy-five monks between the ages of seven and forty from all over the region. Three years later, there were 560 village temples and over 7,000 monks and novices in Sipsongpanna. Most villages had their own local temples, and Wat Pajay supervised them.

In many villages where the crumbling state education system failed minority students, the temple was the only place to study. Some Tai Lüe parents preferred the temples to the public schools anyway, because in public schools Tai Lüe children were taught that the Hans were more advanced and minorities were backward. In the temples they heard about Buddhism and Tai Lüe history, learned to read the old Tai Lüe script, and had the high status of holy men of learning. Through an agreement with the local schools, novice monks attended public school in the morning and temple school in the afternoon. At eighteen or nineteen, novices could leave monastic life or take all the vows and become fully ordained monks.

Those who chose ordination also took on teaching or administrative responsibilities at the temple. At any time they were free to leave temple life to marry and find secular jobs; local girls sometimes teased them, asking when they planned to defrock.

As I stood in the temple courtyard waiting for the verdict, a teenage monk, slim and pale, strolled up and began to chat shyly in English. "How do you do?" he asked, smiling. Another monk hovered a few feet away, listening. "Fine, thank you," I responded. The listening monk literally gasped. Another teenage monk walked up and whispered to him. Suddenly there was a crowd of novices around us, twenty short, gentle bald boys in robes, like a small flock of orange birds. The monk and I chatted in our fragments of English, Chinese, and Thai until the senior monk emerged from his quarters and uttered a few sharp words. The orange robes flew and in seconds all of the novices were absorbed in sweeping, selling incense, and copying manuscripts. The senior monk introduced me to a somewhat fierce-looking young monk in rimless glasses. No one in the temple spoke English, but this twenty-two-year-old, who had just returned to Sipsongpanna from college, spoke Chinese better than anyone else in the temple, he said. Classes would begin tomorrow. The matter of payment was waved off as beneath discussion.

In the early days of these Chinese-style Tai Lüe–language lessons, when my teacher stood sternly in front of a blackboard with a pointer while I obediently squeezed into a child's wooden desk and copied the loops of Tai Lüe letters, we all observed a strained politeness. I certainly had never met a Buddhist monk and worried I would inadvertently do something offensive. My teacher had never met a foreign woman and worried likewise, probably about inadvertently saying something politically inappropriate. In Tibet, just a few hundred miles to the north, Buddhist monks were jailed for expressing a desire for independence from China or for having too much contact with sympathetic American activists. The Tai Lüe monks, like my teacher, sometimes contorted themselves to avoid giving that impression. They daily submitted to government supervisory bodies, gave tours to visiting government dignitaries to show off China's new tolerance of religion, and passed their days in a blizzard of forms reporting on their activities.

The novices, however, felt no such constraints. When I arrived for class each morning, a young novice swinging on the front gate called out, "*Mae galaa bawk ma laew!*"—"Mother barbarian has come back!" Dozens of bald boys in orange flocked out of their classrooms in the dormitory building, leaned over the balcony above the temple courtyard, and shouted "hello!" and "herrooh!" with enthusiasm. The smallest novices, boys of eight or nine, swung from the railing like orange-draped monkeys and giggled with delight at the novelty until their teachers yanked them back into the classrooms.

* * *

THINGS WERE NOT moving as quickly with the singers—in fact, they had stalled. After our one evening of recording, when I came back later to ask her questions about the songs or her craft, E Guang seemed uncomfortable and changed the subject. Hoping to build trust, I became a regular at her café, eating there once or twice a week after language classes and trying out newly-learned phrases with her waitresses. E Guang was always warm and friendly. She greeted me pleasantly and then spent most of the meal sitting at other tables with other customers. She and the waitresses taught me the names for Tai Lüe foods: the varieties of fried ferns, steamed bamboo shoots, barbecue, and dipping sauces made of chilies mixed with garlic, tomatoes, peanuts, or olives. Sometimes she invited me to join her family and staff for lunch. But she did not sing again.

At one of these lunches, singers, journalists, and officials from the local culture bureau had a heated debate in Yunnanese and Tai Lüe about the aesthetics of changkhap. Culture bureaus could at their discretion run other projects besides the song-and-dance troupes: during the 1950s and 1960s the Sipsongpanna culture bureau had run a "changkhap opera" troupe that traveled around the prefecture, using performance genres inspired by Beijing opera to perform traditional Tai Lüe oral poetry narratives. These Tai Lüe narratives were shorn of their Buddhist content and "improved" to make their political messages more acceptable.[5]

The culture bureau also ran an association of Tai Lüe oral poets that hosted a biannual competition based on the historical competitions held by the prince of Sipsongpanna; instead of a prince, though, it was the prefectural government that now chose the winners. It emerged from the conversation that at the previous year's biannual competition, the singers who had been chosen winners exemplified a style of changkhap that E Guang and some other singers felt had been altered to suit the government. "They're changing changkhap," she insisted. It was clear from the excitement around the table that this debate was part of an ongoing conversation about aesthetics between singers and educated fans, like the journalists and officials, who were involved in the local scene. When I told these aficionados that I was interested in studying Tai Lüe oral poetry, the first question they usually asked was "What kind?" Not only was the poetry alive, it was a diverse field, with competing genres, regional differences, repertoires, and styles of performance.

This made it even more surprising that I was unable to get into another performance. Sometimes E Guang said in front of others, like the culture bureau officials who often ate at her café, that she was going to take me to visit her old teacher or to meet some other singer. But when the day came, the trip never took place—the old teacher would be feeling under the weather or something else would have come up. She often said, "I never sing anymore. I'm too old. My voice is no good anymore, I can't compete with the younger singers."

Meanwhile, I pursued other angles. The young clerk with the neck ruffle at the guesthouse business center turned out to be Tai Lüe also, and her uncle was a respected singer. She volunteered to arrange a meeting with him. Weeks passed, and the meeting never materialized—the uncle, she apologized, was busy preparing for a wedding.

I mentioned to E La, my Tai Lüe friend from Journey to the East, that I had come to study oral poets but was having trouble finding one. "There are lots of them!" she said in surprise. "They're everywhere!" She offered to introduce me to her favorite changkhap, an older man who had performed for her best friend's son when he was ill. "He sang all night, and I would go away to lie down and sleep, but then I'd wake up and worry that I was missing his singing, so I would go back and listen some more," she remembered. E La spoke with him, and he agreed to meet with me. But when at the appointed time we walked over to the compound where he lived and climbed the stairs to his apartment, no one answered. His neighbor said that he had been called out of town. "That's the way musicians are," E La said. "They get a whim, and they just pick up and go."

Everyone was polite and friendly, and I was being fed to excess, but the field research that had begun so easily had now become like a long walk toward a receding horizon. It was true, as E La said, that oral poets were everywhere; but somehow, when approached, they melted away and vanished. Unlike in some other parts of the world, here oral traditions had not vanished; but they were hidden in the shadows, screened from the direct gaze of outsiders, and researching them was like trying to grasp clouds. How had I failed to establish rapport? What had I done wrong? The older poets seemed nervous, as if there were something dangerous about singing the old songs.

* * *

WHILE THE OLDER singers seemed friendly but turned out to be conservative, though, the young monks who had begun so formally soon turned out to be more open. One day, I sat down with my monk teacher and opened the novices' Tai Lüe–language primer. Studying Tai Lüe in Chinese was a laborious process. Our only text was the novices' primer, which contained only moral platitudes such as "Don't do evil"—not very helpful when trying to communicate with E Guang. Sometimes when my teacher explained a word in Chinese, I still did not understand it and had to look it up in a Chinese-English dictionary. At times we spent twenty minutes with various dictionaries, charades, and drawings until the meaning was conveyed. Without our respective senses of humor and mutual stubbornness, the language classes would never have lasted.

This time, my teacher, sitting down across the coffee table from me and setting two glasses of hot water before us, asked if I had a computer at home in the United States. I did, but it was not like the Chinese computers I had seen so far. "I have a Macintosh," I said. Not knowing the Chinese term, I drew the familiar logo in my notebook.

"Oh, an Apple," he said, brightening. "Same as us."

"You have an Apple?" I asked doubtfully. The monks' quarters were spartan—a single light bulb hanging overhead, no running water above the ground floor, ratty mosquito nets over worn bunk beds inherited from school dormitories. For the past month, the city had shut off the water supply to the temple, so the novices had to walk to a nearby village and bathe in the homes of lay supporters. The greatest asset the monks had was a wide vista of the valley. Few people in China had such a fashionable thing as a Macintosh, and certainly not those in an impoverished backwater like this.

He stood up and beckoned, pushing his glasses up the bridge of his nose, hitching his robe on his shoulder, and loping quickly down the hall in rubber sandals. I followed him to a small room. In it, surprisingly, were a new carpet and air conditioning. The walls were decorated with color images of dharma wheels printed on a laser printer and a calendar from Thailand. Two monks were standing over two brand-new Power Macs attached to a printer and a color scanner. Languid Thai pop music wafted from one of the CD drives. I wai'ed to the monks, who were preoccupied with the printer. One wore a jaunty cap, and underneath this he was scratching his shaved head. He said something in Tai Lüe to my teacher, who explained, "He keeps sending it to print, but nothing comes out." The monks pulled out a chair for me and clustered around.

I checked the only thing I knew, which was the Chooser. It turned out that the printer had not been selected. I did this, we sent the document to print, and out came a page of Tai Lüe Buddhist scripture. "Oho," said the monk in the cap. With one blow, I had established myself as unofficial tech support to the Buddhist temple, required, always politely, to fix printers, computers, televisions, video players, and, on one occasion, to set the alarm on the abbot's new digital watch. For performing all of those tasks I was gravely thanked.

Most of these electronic gadgets were gifts from businessmen in Thailand, who saw giving such presents as meritorious deeds. Some of the Sipsongpanna monks who had studied in Thai seminaries had picked up basic software skills. Businessmen in Thailand, learning of the monks' interest, had shipped a few Macs over the borders. A friend of the monks had passed along a few disks containing a font developed in Kengtung, Burma, which enabled them to print in the old Tai Lüe script. Using this font, they had begun a small-scale publishing project, typesetting the novices' primer, a few old scriptures, and a calendar for the temple.

But the donors had simply dumped the computers and left; apparently no one had thought of providing the monks with basic computer and troubleshooting skills, still less of teaching them to read English, the language of the software and all the related instructional handbooks. Nor had anyone explained the difference between legitimate and pirated software. Sometimes the computers crashed because of viruses picked up from pirated Thai CDs. When that happened, these unworldly men simply reinstalled the software or put something from the system folder into the trash and deleted it. Communicating about all this with our equally minimal Chinese skills or, worse, with a Tai Lüe primer that only taught moral platitudes, was a challenge with which we struggled for some time. Once I was called in to look at a Macintosh that displayed icons for seven hard drives, and when I tried to fix it I produced only the ominous symbol of the unhappy Mac. "*Dai laew* [it's dead]," sighed the monk.

* * *

IN TEACHING ME the old Tai Lüe script and getting the means to publish their own documents in it, the monks were quietly striking a blow at government control of ethnic culture. In the 1950s, the government announced that the old script was unwieldy and set out to reform it. Until the temple got into the act with their Macintoshes, the result of these efforts was a decrease in literacy in the minority script and a generation cut off from their own written traditions.

The old Tai Lüe written alphabet is complex; it has over sixty letters, and even those expert in the script disagree about exactly how many there are (fig. 12). It is almost identical to the script used by Tai Khuns in Kengtung, Shan State, and closely resembles the alphabets of northern Laos and the Lanna kingdom of northern Thailand. Written on palm leaves and parchment, recopied from one generation to the next, the legacy of texts written and transcribed by monks includes the Pali canon of Theravada Buddhism, from

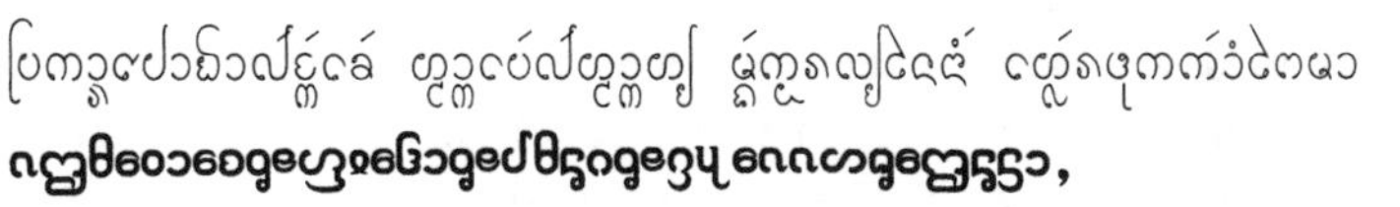

12 *Old Tai Lüe script (above) and new Tai Lüe script (below).*

which the script was adapted. It also includes texts on medicine, astronomy, history, literature, philosophy, and changkhap poetry. Because historically it has been taught in temples, for the most part only Tai Lüe monks and former monks are able to read and write it. In the past, women were not generally taught the script, though some did learn it from male relatives.

Official Chinese rhetoric often refers to presumptive low levels of literacy among all border peoples, without distinction. This was often said to be because of flaws in their scripts, as well as flaws in the pre-"Liberation" educational systems. In 1954 Ma Hsueh-liang explained this in an article, under a section titled "Unsuitable Written Languages":

> There are other minority nationalities with some form of written language. . . . In general they are defective and require improvement. . . . Soon [this] will be accomplished, helping the minorities to raise their culture to a new level as part of the progressive culture of the whole Chinese people and of the peoples of the world.[6]

Thus scripts like those of the Tai Lüe, Tibetans, Uyghurs, and others were banned and replaced with new, "simplified" scripts created by linguists to facilitate literacy. Other ethnic minorities who had historically been nonliterate had new scripts invented for them. In Yunnan, language teams, working with members of the Tai elite, came up with a simplified Tai Lüe alphabet ("*xin Daiwen*") that had fewer letters than the traditional alphabet. This became the official language, to be written on street signs and used in government documents alongside the simplified Chinese script.

Given the lack of access to Tai Lüe historical records (none are archived in China), it is difficult to assess how widespread literacy was in Sipsongpanna before 1949. American missionary William Clifton Dodd, who was literate in Tai, reported a high degree of literacy during his first visit there in 1897. He traveled along the Mekong Delta with copies of his Tai-language translation of the Bible and found the Tai Lüe of Sipsongpanna to be avid readers:

> Never before, in any place, have I met such receptivity, as well as such unbridled curiosity. . . . They take books, they beg books, they clamor for books.[7]

In Sipsongpanna he interviewed a local headman, who reported that "of the Lu [sic] of his district, one-third of the men could read, one-third could barely read, and one-third could not read at all. Only one woman, his wife, could read."[8] If these estimates were representative of the region, we could speculate that overall literacy in Sipsongpanna might have been roughly comparable to the literacy rates among Hans during the same period. Evelyn Rawski estimates that throughout China in the late Qing between one-half and one-third of school-age males had basic literacy.[9] In previous eras of Chinese imperial history, because of lack of access to education, literacy among Chinese-speakers was probably far lower. Given the temple education system, it seems likely that Tai Lüe literacy was actually relatively high, and certainly higher than the Chinese government has reported.

It is clear that the new Tai Lüe script has not promoted increased literacy. Many Tai Lües note that the state has published almost nothing in the new script, making it in effect useless. The twice-weekly four-page newspaper, *Xishuangbanna bao*, is one exception. Public pressure caused the *Xishuangbanna bao* to switch back to old Tai Lüe script during the 1990s before returning to the new Tai Lüe script in 1995 in response, reportedly, to pressure from the provincial government. In 1997, some Tais believed that the newspaper would switch back to the old Tai Lüe script again and were trying to establish a publishing house to produce books in old Tai Lüe; they have not yet been successful. Worse, many Tai Lües pointed out what they saw as government hypocrisy: despite officially promoting the new Tai Lüe script for over forty years, the state had never produced a dictionary for it. At the main temple in Jinghong, Tai Lüe Buddhist monks succeeded in compiling a modest dictionary for the old Tai Lüe script in 2000. Two years later, after a long political struggle with the provincial government, the dictionary was published in Kunming.

Some educated Tai Lües told me that they had never been properly taught the new script and so could not read it: "They only ever taught us new Tai script for one hour a week in secondary school," said one young government official. "I just never really learned it. Anyway, it doesn't have any use," because nothing is published in it. Many noted that those literate in the new script could not read the old script, so that literacy in the new script in effect cuts younger Tai Lües off from their own written traditions. There is no library or archive in China that houses books in the old Tai Lüe script published before 1949.

Today, the politics of language shapes class and status in Sipsongpanna. Most residents of larger towns, especially Jinghong, speak a common local version of the provincial dialect of Mandarin, *Jinghonghua*, or "Jinghong-ese." Tai villagers are more likely to speak Tai only, which itself has several dialects in neighboring towns, but many young village children, surrounded by Chinese-language television, radio, and music, can understand Tai but not speak or read it. Sipsongpanna residents who work in the tourist industry or for the government tend to be those with better education who speak and read standard Mandarin. But as a result of controversial government interventions in the minority alphabet, few Tai Lües are literate in any form of their own language.

In sum, the early government language policy was probably motivated by idealism and the goal of promoting widespread literacy. But if the reforms are aimed at aiding ethnic minorities, and ethnic minorities overwhelmingly reject the reforms, why continue them? The state's dogged adherence to the new Tai Lüe script in the face of widespread opposition, combined with the lack of any archive for classical texts, suggests to many in Sipsongpanna a cynical effort by the state to create *illiteracy* by promoting a new alphabet designed to become obsolete.[10] In recent years, the Tai Lüe script written on street signs in Jinghong has been removed. Tai Lüe officials report that fewer government documents are published even in the new Tai Lüe script. These moves have only fueled local fears of a conspiracy by the state to eradicate their language.

Intentionally or otherwise, through their involvement in script reform, publishing, and censorship, officials undermined ethnic institutions and written traditions to effectively create a semi-literate border people. This may have enhanced Beijing's role as a bearer of Chinese civilization to the borderlands, but it also created widespread resentment in this region, which in turn fueled the revival of the Buddhist temple.

* * *

DESPITE THE MACINTOSH problems, the Wat Pajay computer room had become one of the temple's hidden hearts and a gathering place for young Tai Lües interested in starting something new.

There was something different about the temple, an atmosphere that made it pleasant. For one, it was quiet—free of the sounds of karaoke halls or construction that filled the rest of Jinghong. Entering the grounds, it was as if the bustle and stress of town life fell away. The hill got the best of the cool breezes. Everyone seemed more relaxed, happier, and more polite there. Villagers passed through, often coming to visit with monks they knew, to ask them to chant a prayer for someone with an illness, to give them donations, to discuss a village conflict or to take a rest from them. Young men sometimes stayed for a few days to recover from a hangover or heartbreak. Old men who had been forced to leave monastic life in the 1960s and 1970s came to stroll the grounds, repaint and restring the temple's old ritual drums, or teach the novices. And many people came to use the computers. One Tai Lüe language class was cancelled because my teacher was designing a poster with a local low-level Tai Lüe official, Aye Soong.[11] I sat on the wicker sofa in the computer room and struggled to read the words on the poster. The monks giggled at my pronunciation.

"We're having a concert," explained the monk in the hat. "Tai Lüe–language pop songs. Will you come?"

"Where will it be?"

"Here," said my teacher, pointing out the window at the temple courtyard.

The meaning of this gradually became clear. On my way home, I stopped by a shop next to the temple entrance and noticed a tape unlike the others being sold there. It didn't have Chinese characters and pictures of pretty girls singing the "Xishuangbanna, My Hometown" touropop; this cassette was printed in old Tai Lüe script and had a photo of a young man in modern clothes holding a guitar. I bought it and listened to it at the guesthouse and found the music was catchy—a slow, languorous pop melody sung by a young man with a synthesizer, bass, and guitar. I took it in to show to my teacher.

"Where did you get this?" he said in surprise. "It's Aye Sam!"

"Who is Aye Sam?"

"He is a new Tai Lüe pop singer. He sings in our Tai language."

An ethnic minority pop singer was totally unheard-of in China. "He sings his own songs? He writes them himself? In Tai Lüe?"

My teacher grinned. "He writes some, and some are written by a monk here at Wat Pajay."

"How can a monk write songs? I thought monks took a vow at ordination never to sing." I had found this one of the more memorable vows.

He seemed annoyed. "It's perfectly fine to write song lyrics. He never sings in public." Then he smiled again. "But sometimes he sings here when only we monks can hear him, without other people around."

"What are the songs about?"

He picked up the tape. "There are lyrics in here—actually, we printed them on our computer. You could use this to study Tai." We were both tiring of the novices' primer. "This song is 'Sao Tai bai fon Muang Haw.'" He wrote out the lyrics in Tai Lüe, and we worked through the words together, as he explained each word in Chinese and I wrote it down in English. The title read "Tai girl goes to dance in Muang Haw." We had learned the word "Muang," translated as "Meng" in Chinese—it could mean city or state, depending on the context. "Haw" meant "Han Chinese." But "Muang Haw"?

"Muang Haw is the place where Han people live, like Shanghai or Beijing or the rest of China. Kunming is also in Muang Haw. Some people say that even downtown Jinghong is becoming Muang Haw because so many Han people have moved here," he said. "But I say, not yet. It's still Muang Tai."

"So the song is about Tai girls who go to dance in China?"

"Many Tai girls do this. They go away to dance in the big cities and they never come back. They marry a Han and they stay there, and they forget how to speak our Tai language."

Slowly, we translated the song lyrics:

> The Tai girl is going to dance in the Han region
> Because she wants to be with her Tai boyfriend.
> Don't go live so far away
> Don't go live so far away
> Lovely Tai girl, wherever you go, don't forget Tai
> No matter how far away you live,
> Don't forget the Tai language, or our Tai region, where we were born.
> The Tai girl is going to live in the Han region,
> But she comes back to flirt with Tai boys.
> Don't forget our Tai spoken language
> Don't forget our Tai spoken language
> No matter where this guy goes, he will never forget you,
> No matter how far away this guy lives,
> He will never forget the girl from the Tai region.
> In Muang Sipsongpanna, the Tai Khun people are moving forward
> And developing in every way, isn't it true?[12]
> But in Sipsongpanna, you can see more and more often,
> All these girls are moving away,
> And soon there will be none at all living in the Tai region,
> None in the Tai region.[13]

Like this one, a number of Aye Sam's songs had social themes. Most were love ballads, such as the lament "Amla, sao Muang Long" (Farewell, Muang Long girl).[14] One or two were humorous drinking songs, like "Viang viang mao lao," which described a bunch of drunken Tai boys stumbling around a county market checking out the young women selling produce there. One or two songs dealt implicitly with social issues, like "Panna geut bin" (Born in Panna), which mused, "Young men and women all want to leave. . . . Our people, our ethnic group, our home villages where we were born. . . . But still the Mekong River ebbs and flows." Aye Sam had a sweet voice, but on the one or two occasions when I saw him at the temple, he turned out to be the image of a hard-edged rocker in person: unruly hair, Burmese tattoos, and a gravelly voice, a diminutive Bruce Springsteen.

Aye Sam was reluctant to speak to me, so I asked to interview the monk who wrote the songs. My teacher frowned at the coffee table the way he did anytime I asked him a question about Buddhism, the government, or anything he didn't like. "I'll ask," he concluded. Some months later, Dubi Gang agreed to be interviewed under a pseudonym and with my teacher present.[15]

Dubi Gang began writing songs while studying at a temple in Thailand, he said. He had heard *lukthoong* songs in the northern Thai dialect, a kind of socially conscious country music closely related to local folk-song traditions. The northeastern Thai dialect is similar to Tai Lüe, and having grown up in China, Dubi Gang was struck by the novel sound of contemporary pop songs in his own language. Why had he never heard anything like this in Sipsongpanna? he asked himself. The monk began translating the northeastern Thai songs into Tai Lüe for fun. Then he tried writing one of his own.

As he began working on this, he said, he started to see it as a project that would be "educational, not just music." Like some of the other monks at Wat Pajay, Dubi Gang felt some frustration at the ways that Tai Lüe culture was staged by the state. "The dancers you see now are not performing for us but for tourists. These dances are not Tai culture. The songs are not Tai songs—the dances are modern and the clothes are not what we used to wear." He pulled out a photograph album with images of villagers dancing for Buddhist and other holiday festivals and referred back to the cultural shows for tourists:

> That is not our real culture. We still have a real culture in the villages, which you see at Buddhist ceremonies. . . . But schools do not teach

this culture, so it will disappear, and only the old people will know and keep it.

Like some other Tai Lüe monks, Dubi Gang was concerned about the growing pressure in Sipsongpanna to assimilate into the Chinese mainstream and the lack of pop culture in Tai Lüe to compete with the onslaught of Chinese martial arts films and Cantonese pop songs. The lack of Tai Lüe culture, he said, reinforced a sense of inferiority and low self-esteem among China's ethnic minorities. "Young Tais go to karaoke halls and sing in Chinese. This is harmful to one's own culture and one's self-image," he said. "I want to use my songs to teach."

By creating a hip, contemporary culture in the old Tai Lüe script, Dubi Gang aimed to build the self-esteem of local youth. This, he stressed, would help Sipsongpanna to develop more quickly, strengthening both Yunnan province and China as a whole.

It was an argument carefully modulated to address any possible charges of ethnic separatism. While the government had declared itself committed to preserving ethnic minority cultures, in fact it was only committed to those elements it sanctioned as contributing to economic development and modernization, such as theme parks. Dubi Gang and his friends were accepting these rules but stretching the definition of development. They were not only reviving old things, such as the script and the temple; their aim was to create a new, modern Tai Lüe culture that included Macintoshes and pop music. Thus they were using the state rhetoric of national "modernization and development" to promote ethnic empowerment.

Dubi Gang had written songs about social problems: the one about the Tai Lüe dancer, and others on HIV/AIDS, and the growing problem of the traffic of Tai Lüe women and girls into the Thai sex industry. "We are spiritual people, and according to tradition we should not really do what we are doing," or writing songs, he said. "But if I don't do it, who will? If I can help our culture, I have to do it."

A few days later, walking out of the dorm after class, I happened to meet the abbot, who was standing in the courtyard with a group of monks. The temple's abbot was a portly man, in contrast to the slender monks, and some of the senior monks liked to joke in private about his bulk. They also spoke with admiration of him as an orator. Fleeing the Cultural Revolution, his family had taken him over the border into Shan State when he was a child. He ordained in Kengtung and studied at a prominent old temple where he became well known for his sermons. When Wat Pajay was rebuilt in 1990, Tai Lües in Sipsongpanna asked for him to be their new abbot.

The monk with the hat had given me a Tai Lüe name, Fragrant Lotus, a reference to a metaphor about the beginning of a new Buddhist era. The abbot called out, "Fragrant Lotus, how are your studies progressing?" He pointed out to the other senior monks standing around him that it was unusual for a person of another ethnicity to study Tai Lüe. My presence as a student of the language was often part of this kind of Tai Lüe proselytizing in favor of language revival. The abbot expressed appreciation for the technical help and mentioned that he faced some opposition to some of his work. "They would like us to sit in the temple and chant sutras," he said, in heavily accented Chinese. "But look at us, we are all young men. We want to do something for our society." He shook his head. "Every time they look at me, they think of Tibet, but Sipsongpanna is not the same."

***

I WAS STILL making no progress with E Guang or the other singers, so I began to look further into the pop-song movement and started to discover its transnational sources. On a sunny afternoon, I took the juddering bus to a nearby town to meet with one of the brains behind Tai pop music, Aye Nawn. The bus let me off in a dusty market square, and I followed directions given over a cell phone to a temple nearby.

The old temple was a hive of bustling senior citizens. A thin, elderly man with a bent back was repaving the front walkway, scraping the cement he had mixed back and forth with a rake. Another man crouched, retouching the red stenciled paintings of flowers that circled the temple's indoor columns. Another retiree had spread out some old paper puppets and was watching as young novices squatted in their sandals, cutting out new puppets with scissors. A Tai Lüe journalist had recently written an essay about this in the *Xishuangbanna bao*. In certain villages around Sipsongpanna, the journalist observed, senior citizens were setting aside one day a week to meet at the temple and do good works. They swept the building floor, did minor repairs, retouched the old Buddhist murals, and played with the novices. These activity days got older folks out of the house and eased their isolation, he wrote, when young people were often too busy working to care for their parents the way they did in the old days.

Aye Nawn emerged from inside the main hall engrossed in conversation with an elderly man. He was a dynamic man in his late twenties, impossibly thin, with a boyish, enthusiastic smile that had been the undoing of a number of Tai Lüe women. He greeted me cheerfully and led the way past an elder who was putting a gaggle of small novices through a prayer recitation. We sat on straw mats spread out under the temple porch, where a grandmotherly lady brought us glasses of tea. "We've just started fixing up this temple, so I'm sorry we don't have any chairs. But these elders won't mind if we share the shade with them." The group of five or six elders sitting on a straw mat under the shade of the temple eaves slipped aside, making room for us, bringing glasses of water to us, and stayed close enough to listen in to our conversation.

According to Dubi Gang, the Tai Lüe pop-music movement had begun with four men in their thirties: Dubi Gang, who wrote the songs; Aye Sam, who sang them; and Aye Nawn and Aye Soong, two junior government officials who organized the concerts and recordings. Against the depression and boredom common among Tai Lües in Sipsongpanna, Aye Nawn's optimism radiated outward, inspiring others to action.

"So," he said, settling onto the mat. "What would you like to know?"

"Can you tell me about the origins of the Tai pop-song movement?"

"The origins of Tai pop songs . . ." he said. "To do that, I have to go into some history."

Sipsongpanna Tai Lüe pop song, he said, had sprung out of the expansion of cultural networks back across the borders of China and Southeast Asia. As a result of increasing trade across the borders, the cultural field in this minority region of China began to expand to accept Southeast Asian influences and reshaped itself behind the scenes of the state-sponsored development projects.

It had begun, Aye Nawn said, with the Cultural Revolution, when traditional oral poetry was banned, as was singing of any kind except for a handful of official songs praising the Party. But Tais continued to sing secretly in the villages. Gradually, songs began to float up from across the borders.

In this period, as Craig Lockhard charts, Thai pop music was becoming increasingly "identified with mass-based sociopolitical movements seeking change."[16] During the 1970s, pop groups like Caravan and Carabao emerged, linked to Thailand's left-wing student democracy movements. These groups had in turn risen out of the socially conscious song genre *lukthoong* ("child of the fields"), which sprang up in impoverished northeast Thailand. "These songs," writes Lockhard, "have a simpler style and utilize the northeastern vernacular for easy communication with the target audience. Many musicians come from backgrounds in folk music such as *molam*," a form of oral narration in Thailand and Laos very close to Sipsongpanna's changkhap poetry. Lockhard notes, "The songs describe life in the countryside, including both romantic nostalgia and the difficult realities facing many peasants."[17]

Meanwhile, in Burma, Tais (or Shans, as they are known there) were listening to their own harder-edged ethnic rock music, including the Mick Jagger of Shan State, Sai Mao. Sai Mao was a legend, a hard-living man known for his love of young girls, loud music, glitzy floor shows, and pan-Tai pride. One of his songs, written by a friend and demanding that Burma keep its promise of ethnic independence, got him imprisoned by the Burmese military junta for two years. This only enhanced his status to many of his fans. By the early 1980s, Sai Mao was a Tai icon in the Mekong Delta. Bootleg copies of his cassettes began to appear in Tai homes and in village marketplaces in Laos, Thailand, and eventually Sipsongpanna.

Temples were central to much of this activity in Thailand, Burma, and Laos. Lockhard notes that lukthoong was also performed in concerts at temple fairs, to crowds that stood waiting for hours to hear the singers.[18] In these regions, it was the temple's job to promote education and culture, sometimes by staging performances of oral poetry, puppetry, or folk theater. The sight of a Buddhist monk hefting a camcorder or setting up a stage for a pop band, while anomalous to a Chinese or Western gaze, was a common one along the Mekong Delta. On pirated cassettes, the Thai and Burmese Shan pop and rock songs had slipped into Sipsongpanna gradually, in the bags of traders and travelers moving among Thailand, Laos, Burma, and China.

Aye Nawn received some of these tapes from traveling friends and bought others in local vegetable markets. He remembered sitting in a café with his high school sweetheart, asking the café owner to play their Sai Mao tape over and over again as he and his girlfriend sang along. As Sipsongpanna modernized, Chinese-language music from Beijing, Hong Kong, Taiwan, and the United States, flooded the Jinghong music shops, and the new Chinese state-sponsored touropop began to echo nightly from hotels, theme parks, and restaurants. Thai and Burmese Tai-language pop was an alternative to the mainstream music. Chinese and foreign tourists were hearing one set of songs in the theme parks and restaurants, but local Tai Lües were singing a different set of songs for themselves.

Listening to the pop music dribbling into Yunnan through trade routes across Burma began to give people ideas. In the early 1990s, a musical explosion took place in the western villages near the town of Meng Hai. Individual singers began emerging, guys who sang with a Tai Lüe banjo, the *ting*, and who wrote their own words and melodies.

Aye Nawn, Dubi Gang, and Aye Soong, all buddies from high school, had been having conversations until late into the night about their desire to jump-start a Tai Lüe cultural rebirth. When they heard Aye Sam sing at a dinner one night, something clicked. Aye Sam put together the New Star Band, a bunch of schoolteachers and farmers who "came out of the fields, picked up the guitars, and began to play," said Aye Nawn. Dubi Gang wrote the songs and the others organized some recordings, photographing and designing the cassette covers themselves, distributing the cassettes to local shops.

The first tape sold well. But when Aye Nawn approached the prefectural culture bureau with the idea of doing a more professional recording, (he) met opposition, he said:

> We waited and waited for help from the government for a long time, and they didn't do anything. They just managed the state song-and-dance troupe; they had no interest in doing more. Finally, we turned to the temple and the temple stepped in—not with a religious agenda, but with the intention of preserving and developing Tai culture.

With the help of the temple, Aye Nawn and the others put together the cassette with Aye Sam's photograph on it that I had bought. Most of the local music stores declined to carry the cassettes, fearing political fallout. But as word got around, the tapes sold quickly. Inevitably, pirated copies began to appear in local vegetable markets, sold alongside the smuggled and pirated cassettes from Burma and Thailand. By early 1997, the tape had been out for six or eight months, and it was played even in the remote villages of the region. In a temple in Meng Zhe, a group of giggling little novices, when asked if they knew any Tai Lüe songs, hid shyly behind a door and belted out the lyrics to an Aye Sam song. The market was huge: there was no local competition.

With cassettes selling out everywhere, Aye Nawn decided to try organizing a pop concert. The first Tai "Woodstock" in December 1997 lasted day and night for three days, and it was attended by thousands of Tai Lües from all over the prefecture.[19] A few Tai Lües had even come from Laos and Burma. Respected changkhap, including E Guang, had been invited to judge the singers and award prizes to the best ones. Initially, the government had opposed the concert and the organizers feared that police would be sent down from Kunming to end it. Then the prefectural government decided to sponsor it—after, some noted wryly, all the legwork had already been done.

Aye Nawn remembered how nervous he was about a Beijing or Kunming crackdown on the day of the concert. "On top of that, rain was forecast for the whole weekend. But when the day came, it suddenly cleared up, as if it were fate. Thousands of people came from all over the prefecture and everyone stayed until two or three in the morning, each night." Aye Nawn concluded, "This experience has given us a real feeling of hope. If we can do this, we can achieve anything we set our minds to."

I asked what he wanted to achieve most. He sighed and shook his head. "I have dreams," he said:

> Someday, I dream I will go into one of those discos in Jinghong, and instead of seeing only a karaoke screen up there and all our Tai youth dancing and singing in Chinese, I dream that they will hear local Tai music, and that you will see both Chinese and classical Tai script rolling across the screen. I don't know if that will ever happen. But if it did, I would know we had made real progress.

Aye Nawn, Aye Soong, and Dubi Gang had called themselves the "Dai Nationality Culture Association of Xishuangbanna," and they had written up a statement that described their hopes for using local cultural projects, like pop-music recordings, as a foundation on which to further economic development. I had had the idea that I could try to find these producers some U.S. funding to help them build their own recording studio in Jinghong. Without permission to use Kunming radio-station recording studios, they had been resorting to all kinds of complicated maneuvers in order to make their tapes.

Aye Nawn and Aye Soong dug up a copy of the statement to see if we could turn it into a grant proposal of some kind. Sitting in the Journey to the East café, Aye Nawn and Aye Soong described their ambitious early plans for the association, which included formal memberships, annual dues, and regular meetings. But they had abandoned the plan as unworkable without the sanction of a government bureau. Spontaneous associations are illegal in China. Older Tai Lües had cautioned them against moving forward.

"The culture association is never going to happen. Everyone is so scared, especially old people! What are they afraid of?"

"They're afraid of Tibet," I suggested. "Or the former Soviet Union."

Aye Soong shook his head in irritation. "This is not Tibet or the Soviet Union. Sipsongpanna is completely different."

This was the mantra of Tai Lües. Around us the café had emptied out. Recently, the numbers of foreign tourists, which could ebb and flow inexplicably, had abruptly dropped off. Still, the storefront was invitingly full of soft yellow light, the hanging lamps covered with coconut shells, most of the batik-covered tables empty. Anulan, E La, and one of the male dancers from the Manting Road restaurants were all sitting in the café kitchen, cracking sunflower seeds, watching Chinese soap operas, and making witchy jokes about TV stars being sluts.

"I'll try my best to get some funding," I said, half-joking, waving their statement over the table. "But I hope there's nothing in this that says that the Tai Culture Association wants an independent nation, because if so, I'll get in trouble."

This was saying the unsayable. The two men leaned back on the wicker sofa and laughed. "Don't worry, don't worry," said Aye Nawn, waving one hand and wiping away tears of laughter with the other.

"Of course, we've discussed it," said Aye Soong, suddenly serious. "Do you think we don't know what happens in the rest of the world? But if Sipsongpanna were an independent nation, we would be like Laos or Nepal. We'd be completely on our own, surrounded by bigger countries. No one would care what happens to us."

Aye Nawn grinned. "Aside from Fragrant Lotus, of course."

"An independent nation would be a big hassle," said Aye Soong.

"And who would run it?" he asked Aye Nawn.

"Oh, what a fight that would be, ga," said Aye Nawn to Aye Soong. "Oh, a real fight."

I joked, "How about you guys?"

They both grinned, but Aye Nawn shook his head. "There was a time when we thought about things like that, but things are changing in China. Look at what we've managed to accomplish with the Tai Lüe music. With China's reform and opening up, we have some hope that we can make things better for our people as part of China's development." He concluded, "And if we're right, what a great example that would set for other minorities in China, or for Tais in Burma."

"We really feel for the Tais in Burma, their situation is very bad," said Aye Soong. "Look at what happened to Tais in Shan State who tried to establish their own country. They are treated terribly."

"Yes, so if we're successful over here in Yunnan, then maybe that will inspire the Shans, or other minority groups in China, and give them hope."

* * *

THE CROWD OF Tai Lüe villagers surged forward as I scrambled on my knees in the dust to protect the tape recorder and microphone, aimed up at the lip of a handmade wooden stage. I leaned back against the pressure of the bodies in an effort to shield the instruments from stampeding fans. The crowd smelled of sweat and dust. Little boys in long-billed baseball caps and small girls in long skirts, lipstick, and earrings crammed around, torn between staring at the white person with the strange equipment and at the big stage. The wooden platform was festooned with strings of Christmas tree lights and potted plants, against a backdrop decorated with pastel paper cutouts of Buddhist wheels, lotus flowers, and old Tai Lüe script (fig. 13). Their mothers and grandmothers, standing behind them in sarongs and buns, ordered the kids back. The monk with the hat stood in the middle of the crowd, aiming a bulky temple camcorder at the stage. Above us, onstage, a short, muscular man with long hair and a string of blue tattoos on his left arm was singing in Tai Lüe:

> Your father, he is Tai
> Your mother, she is Tai
> Why do you speak the language of others?
> Your children, they are Tai
> Your grandchildren, they are Tai
> Why do you teach them the language of others?
> Tais should speak the Tai language
> Tais should learn the Tai alphabet
> When you were born, you were Tai
> When you die, you will be Tai
> And in the next world, we will all be Tai.

This was the second Tai pop concert and it was being held in the courtyard of Wat Pajay, on the anniversary of China's granting of

13 *The New Star Band performs at the second Sipsongpanna pop concert. Aye Sam is second from left on electric guitar.*

"religious freedom" to its citizens, the annual time when a class of novices passed their annual examinations.

A crowd of thousands packed the courtyard, though the only advertising the organizers had done was a handful of posters like the ones I had seen in the computer room. Again, word of mouth—in Tai Lüe—had done it all, bringing thousands from around the prefecture.

E Guang climbed onstage to an ovation. She wore a dazzling blue lamé dress, gold jewelry and makeup, her hair in its Tai Lüe bun decorated with plastic flowers and ribbons. She began with an a cappella song in the genre called "*Heaui heaui naw*" for its opening phrase, literally "Hey hey now." This genre is usually sung by a woman as part of an improvised duet with a man in which they challenge each other. The "Hey hey now" genre of Tai changkhap song is usually gentle, lyrical, and thoughtful, but some singers use the "Hey hey now" songs to sing laments about men or to improvise social commentary. Typically, their rendering in Chinese videos and recordings is as lyrical love songs performed by pretty girls, but they are not always so simple in practice; in the hands of a skilled singer, they are an invitation to a duel. E Guang sang:

Hey hey now,
At sunset, when the sky turns yellow,
We two agreed to meet in a certain place.
I have waited since sunset for you,
Waited for too long, looking around, waiting,
I did not see you,
I stood up a while, then sat down again,
Took a palm tree leaf to sit on in the grass,
And stayed until it turned yellow and withered.
The leaf I had wrapped rice in
Turned bitter and yellow,
The salt I had wrapped up turned brown.[20]
Why have you still not come out of the house?

Meanwhile, a man of about the same age, accompanied by a few women, walked backstage and asked the monk who was engineering the sound for a microphone. The monk, puzzled, turned it over to him, and encouraged him to join E Guang onstage. The man with the microphone declined with a wave of his hand and sat down backstage, where E Guang could not see him. After another line or two from E Guang, he interrupted with a sung lyric:

Hey hey now,
E Guang, you great lady changkhap,
You are as lovely as a cucumber flower.

The audience laughed and began to call for him to come onto the stage. E Guang looked around to see where the voice was coming from but could not see the singer. She smiled wryly and responded to his challenge, inviting him to join her onstage. The man responded: E Guang should not sit alone waiting for him; like the banana leaf she used to wrap her rice, her bloom would also begin to fade.

E Guang sweetly asked again why her challenger did not dare to join her onstage:

Why are you singing from a place where I can't see you?
Brother, perhaps I could fall in love with you [if I could see you],

You should not hide in the dark and be so shy.
A man should be like water in a village well,
Deep and glimmering, a jewel that emits light for all to admire.
But you—you hide in the dark like a mushroom.

The audience roared. E Guang continued,

Perhaps I won't be able to love you after all,
Perhaps it is not meant to be.

The man responded,

Suppose my wife were to die,
You could come into my home, help me out, and marry me.

The woman sitting beside him laughed, cursed, and slapped him. The audience cheered. E Guang said, "All right, all right, that's enough." A changkhap singer who cannot top a sung challenge is defeated. She descended the stage and gave her microphone back to the monk. Her challenger had already disappeared.

E Guang was the best-known changkhap in the region, but women singers had an ambiguous role in Tai Lüe society. While admired universally, they were sometimes criticized by male changkhap who resented their prominence and how the tourism industry had increased the visibility of Tai Lüe women while making men invisible. Monks had organized the new Tai Lüe pop-music concerts and they usually featured male pop singers. Singers like E Guang sometimes expressed frustration with their exclusion from the group of organizers, and then she got up onstage only to be undermined by a rival male singer. Many Tai Lüe songs are, like this one, flirtatious, sometimes sexually explicit improvised duels between male and female singers. Thus a degree of outspokenness was acceptable and expected for successful Tai Lüe women, especially recognized masters like E Guang, but even she could face pressures at home if her husband resented her performing in public. This new space of public expression was emerging in Sipsongpanna, and its parameters and rules were still being defined.

***

ON AN OCCASION like this, even the foreign barbarian had to sing—
there was no way out of it, not after pursuing everyone else with
my tape recorder for months. In a sweaty cotton shirt and jeans, I
was hauled backstage to loom over a gaggle of petite young Tai Lüe
women, slender and shapely in tightly-wrapped flowered sarongs,
high heels, and red rouge. I climbed the ladder onto the stage,
and Aye Sam handed me his electric guitar. Pulling the strap over
my shoulder, I turned to face two thousand Tai Lües. An intake of
breath ran across the sea of black heads filling the dusty courtyard,
and the murmur: "*Mae galaa* ['Mother barbarian']." I began to strum
some opening bars as Aye Sam's New Star Band struggled to back
up the unfamiliar blues tuning and rhythm. There were a few ironies inherent in being a white woman trotted out to join in this
ethnic revival in a region where ethnic minority culture had been
appropriated by Hans—by singing blues, the appropriated music of
African Americans. Perhaps the postcolonial ironies were to blame
for the mixed reception we got. "That *khap galaa* ['barbarian chanting'] sounds sad and angry," commented my monk teacher politely
in our lessons the next day. "Next time, we hope you'll sing in Tai."

I subsequently tried to bring in some foreign pop and rock cassettes to see whether any of them would ignite interesting Tai-funk
fusions, but while the monks listened politely, they were uninter-
ested in songs if they could not understand the lyrics. My teacher fa-
vored James Brown, but was not sure. "Why is he saying 'ow, ow'?"
he asked. "Is someone hurting him?" Lyrics were everything. To an
outsider, Sipsongpanna's pop-music concerts might seem to be a
Western phenomenon, a symptom of the homogenization caused
by globalization, but to leave with this impression would have been
a mistake. In fact, you did not have to dig very far below the surface
here to find a passionate debate about globalization and modernity
with no visible Western referent.

To Bex, the Tai Lüe concerts were dull. "Everyone just stands
around with these stunned expressions," she said. "They just sing
all these Chinese pop songs, don't they, and stand around staring
like they're at a car wreck." It was true that the Tai Lüe words were

sometimes sung to Chinese pop tunes—again, for Tai Lües, melody was only valuable as a rhythm against which to display powerful lyrics. It was also true that in comparison with some of the rock concerts Bex and I had attended in our own countries, with their nudity, mud, and hallucinogens, a Tai Lüe concert seemed tame. But if the Tai Lües looked stunned at those first concerts, it could also have been the tension caused by trying to enjoy music while waiting for that feared police crackdown. These fans actually put our middle-class punks to shame.

* * *

AFTER A FEW more concerts were held in village temples, the atmosphere relaxed, and the shows became informal, friendly exchanges in which members of the audience took turns onstage. There were dozens more concerts in 1998. Gradually, in following years, the slow machinery of the state began to grind, closing down the concerts, one by one. But the songs were already out—people were singing them everywhere.

The situation with E Guang came to a head after a few months. Giving up, I went back to Mr. Dao, the government official, to ask for a new introduction. By now his Yunnanese was becoming more comprehensible to me. He pulled out his address book. "Aye Zai Guang goes down to the countryside all the time, and no one knows more than him about what goes on in the villages," he said while looking up the number, "but watch out, that man has a small drinking problem, ga."

Aye Zai Guang turned out also to have a deep love of the old traditions and to be a devoted socialist, the kind who took personally to heart every official directive about self-sacrificing in order to help impoverished villagers. He spent many months taking me and anyone who felt like joining us to seek out old singers, simply because he loved the fact that anyone might be interested in this art form. But over lunch or dinner Aye Zai Guang did sometimes drink and become quiet and wavery, vanishing behind the dinner table, the image of disappointed idealism. After an excited first interview in an old government office with wooden slats in the windows, he

promised to take me to meet a great oral poet, the best in the prefecture. As we crossed the street from his office together, it began to
look as if we were walking toward E Guang's café.

"We're not going to see E Guang, are we?" I asked.

"Yes, do you know her?" he asked with surprise. "If you do, you
do not need my help—she can take you into the countryside and let
you record many songs."

"I have met her," I answered. "But since she doesn't sing anymore, we have not gone into the countryside together."

"Doesn't sing anymore?" said Aye Zai Guang. "But she sang last
Saturday, she's singing this weekend, and my wife went to hear her
sing yesterday."

We sat in near silence side by side over an awkward dinner at E
Guang's café, with the same group of journalists, folklorists, and
culture bureau officials I had already met many times before. After
an hour or so, one of the group gently advised E Guang that she
should help with research. E Guang flushed, put down the glass she
had been using to join in collective toasts, and delivered a long and
emphatic speech in Tai Lüe. The rest of the table listened in embar-
rassed silence, but I understood none of it. After a few minutes, Aye
Zai Guang and the others raised their glasses for a diplomatic toast
and changed the subject.

I never learned exactly what E Guang had said that night. One
friend explained tactfully, "She didn't understand what you were doing here." Another: "She didn't say anything." A third: "She thought
you were going to steal her recordings and get rich from them in
America." Eventually a clearer picture emerged, though not a single
answer. Accustomed to being paid well, E Guang did not appreciate
not being compensated for the initial performance in her café. My
offer of payment in front of others had obviously had to be declined
for reasons of face. And, didn't everyone know that in China, if you
really wanted to give something, you offered it three times? Perhaps
she had been overwhelmed by all the technical gear I had brought to
that first recording and offended by a gaffe when I had left the tape
recorder on during informal conversation. She was almost certainly
uncomfortable with my probing questions about what she viewed
as an intensely private craft. I had clearly offended her in several

different ways, but, perhaps, like many divas in other countries, E Guang was relatively easy to offend.

This was actually the interpretation given over beers one night by my indignant friend E La. "That E Guang was afraid everyone would laugh at the recordings of her songs in America and say her voice was no good." This was the unlikeliest explanation; even to a novice's ear, E Guang had a unique and powerful voice. Over time, she and I patched things up, and I ate many more dinners at her café with Tai Lüe friends. But by then, it had become clear that there was more than one voice backstage in Sipsongpanna.

***

BY THE TIME the major April holiday, Songkran, rolled around, everyone had become used to the pop concerts. It looked at that time as if the troops were not going to come down from Kunming after all; in fact, the government seemed to be ignoring the whole movement. The novelty had worn off for the crowds who had turned out for the first concert, while for others the pop concerts had become their scene, events they were sure not to miss. Some Tai Lües were starting to organize their own concerts at smaller local temples. A few new bands started to emerge, rivals to Aye Sam's New Star Band.

With some political negotiation, Aye Nawn and his friends succeeded in obtaining permission for the Burmese Tai singer Sai Mao to do a concert tour in Sipsongpanna. He and a few lukthoong musicians from Thailand performed for the week before Songkran in Meng Hai and Jinghong to packed houses of Tai Lües. E Guang and other changkhap followed around, attending every show. The final concert was held at Wat Pajay. This time about 300 people attended, sitting on the grassy lawn under the stars and trading jokes with the singers onstage.

At about 11 p.m., E Guang and a bevy of female changkhap arrived to claim their turn onstage. Unlike the young rockers of New Star, these women changkhap looked polished and professional, in floor-length lamé gowns and elaborate traditional hairdos. They were good at working the audience, striding across the stage with the mikes and improvising patter, trading witty barbs with the audience. They told the Tai Lüe youth in the audience that they needed to speak Tai Lüe, to be proud of their origins and culture. They dueled with one another in sparkling strings of rhymed prose.

One of the singers was E Lan Gaew, the queen of Chinese touropop, and a gracious singer in her forties who had recently returned home to nurse her ailing mother. For years E Lan Gaew had reigned at the Beijing Minorities Theme Park, making famous recordings of Chinese-language songs about Sipsongpanna including one called "Moonlight on the Wind-Tail Bamboo." The monks put the tape E Lan Gaew had brought with her into the sound system as she ascended the stage in glittering lamé to the brassy accompaniment of "Xishuangbanna, My Hometown."

The song, which she performed with flair, was received with limp and scattered applause. When it was over, one of the men sitting on the lawn in front, made a bit loud with drink, shouted out, "*Khap gam Tai, naw!*" ("Hey, sing in the Tai language!"). E Lan Gaew smiled sweetly and began to sing "Moonlight in the Wind-Tail Bamboo"—in Chinese, again accompanying music on the tape. Someone else shouted, "*Khap gam Tai!*" The cry was taken up in different quarters. E Awn Noy, a popular young changkhap, chimed in: "Big sister, why don't you sing us a song in our Tai language?"

E Lan Gaew apologized: she hadn't prepared a song in Tai Lüe, but she was happy to be back in her hometown. "I took a song-and-dance troupe from the theme park to Japan recently, and we were received warmly. How about if I sing you a Japanese song?" she asked. She started a Japanese song but the cry began again—*khap gam Tai, khap gam Tai* ("sing in Tai"). E Lan Gaew apologized and ceded the stage, defeated. E Guang took up the microphone and began to perform a "Hey, hey now" song in Tai Lüe.

A few songs later, E Awn Noy took the microphone back and began to speak, encouraging the young audience to love and preserve their native tongue, the Mekong River, and Sipsongpanna. Then she curtsied, with one hand gracefully over her heart, head bowed politely, and performed a long, passionate, humorous love song in Tai Lüe. "Your form is so big and strong, like a great Bodhi tree," she sang. "I wish I could take shelter under your arms. Why are you so shy?

Why don't you come out and respond to me, and sing by my side onstage?" The object of the challenge was visible to the whole audience: the abbot, sitting under the shelter backstage, a deep, crimson red covering his face and bald head. Because monks take that vow not to sing he had to keep his silence in public, and so was perhaps defeated by his singing challenger. "*Ya khap dubi!* [Don't sing (about) the monk]!" some younger people called out from the laughing audience. E Awn Noy apologized profusely. She walked offstage, kneeled in front of the abbot, and received his forgiveness.

✳✳✳

AS I BIKED in darkness down the bumpy hill that led from the temple to Manting Road, a group of teen novices raced past on motorcycles, heading home to a nearby village temple. In the light of a heavy full moon, their robes whipped out behind them like wings. The monks and their lay friends had created a cultural and religious movement that was now part of the Yunnan landscape, but how far could it go?

While I bumped along the rutted road, the cassette recorder was wrapped safely in my backpack. The revival of ethnic traditions in the context of a tourism boom created a space for the expression of "coded dissent"—subversive messages delivered under the eyes of the dominator, in ways that the dominators might not recognize. Perry Link had noticed similar approaches among Han Chinese writers in the 1980s:

> Recognizing the leadership's jealous regard for "face" and the dangers of challenging it, writers often attacked by indirection, buffering their criticisms with a layer of what American politicians sometimes call "deniability." This indirection had the added benefit of allowing people who shared a fairly widespread but forbidden view to signal—in public but in code—their tacit comradeship.[21]

Folklorists Joan Radner and Susan Lanser had noted similar strategies in the United States.[22] James Scott calls such messages "hidden transcripts."[23] I suggest that we think of something larger than a message or a transcript: a resistant space that operates below the radar of the state, a backstage area behind the public display. In Sipsongpanna this space was created and boundaries were maintained in several ways.

First, Tai Lües gave "tributary performances": like the dancers in theme parks and restaurants, and like E Guang's initial performance for me, they borrowed from the historical model and sang praise songs for people in power that matched imperial stereotypes about ethnic culture. This ensured that visitors to Sipsongpanna left satisfied, having seen exactly what they wanted to see. Second, they held their biggest events, the ones that could not be hidden, off the tourist map: the pop concerts, and later some of the largest Buddhist festivals, took place not in downtown Jinghong but in small towns. Other events were held in the back of Buddhist temples and in other places where high-ranking officials and most tourists would not be forced to confront them. Third, like Dubi Gang, they used state rhetoric to justify resistant activities, speaking of language revival as assisting in officially approved goals of economic development. Last, but definitely not least, they had found ways to reactivate some of the historical institutions and advantages of the Tai Lüe—the Buddhist temple system, the cross-border exchange networks, the existence of an obscure script that no one else could read—to serve new purposes.

All of these strategies helped the Tai Lüe ethnic revival, but most of the time outright subterfuge was not necessary: As one Tai Lüe put it, "There are two Jinghongs. Hans see the one that they want to see."

The sung exchanges I had recorded the night of the concert had played out all of these larger tensions—the ongoing debate about who and what should be taken to represent Tais to the rest of China and the world at large, the debates about fakeness and realness, and the debates between generations and genders. Not only was there a living Tai Lüe oral poetry, there were multiple poetries, and Tai Lüe culture behind the front-stage display often broke down along age, gender, and other lines. Meanwhile, the conversations in song that took place on that stage, and on other stages like it that year, stretched and increased the social relevance of ethnic tradition even as it was being revived and reinvented.

3

The Oral Poet Laureate

O, cousins from Beijing!
Please, stay a little while.
Look! Every stilt house
gathers up the finest fruits,
steeps the most fragrant Meng Hai tea,
and waits for you to come in and chat.
O, cousins from Beijing!
You bring the greetings of the Party and of Chairman Mao,
And each nationality feels true equality;
It is your warm hands
That dispel the misunderstandings of the old society
and tie us together;
your warm hands
that light a bright lamp in our hearts
so that we can see a brilliant future.
O, cousins from Beijing!
You bring light and hope into Tai family villages,
The forest fills with the rising sound of our grateful song.[1]

WITH AYE ZAI GUANG and some of his friends, local Tai Lüe journalists
and officials who were fans of changkhap oral poetry, I made a series
of trips to Tai Lüe villages around Sipsongpanna. I began gradually
to enter the world of oral poets, moving deeper into a "backstage"
arena of song and debate.

This was a mostly oral world, unlike the dominant world of guidebooks and maps. If text and orality have engaged in a massive battle in human history, it is fair to say that text has won. Our contemporary world is inscribed and circumscribed by the written word: signposts, tax forms, packaging, newspapers, even e-mail, much of it produced by governments and businesses, all mark and guide our experience of reality at every level. Reading the printed word can even be said to be a form of hypnosis, a kind of legal drug that induces visions in the person who consumes it. In the Tai Lüe village network that makes up the border areas of Yunnan province, we found a world where text is seen only occasionally. Some of the oral poets we met were literate in the old Tai Lüe script, and a few knew a smattering of the new Tai Lüe script, but they did not rely on text the way that, for instance, Aye Zai Guang or I did. Their listeners did not hear them passively, the way most of us read books; instead, they commented, cheered, and talked back.

The myth that the literate have promoted in order to justify our total dependence on script is that nonliterate people and orality itself are simpler and less demanding, but such is not the case. The written word is certainly more efficient as a form of mass communication: it is static, easily replicable, portable, and can effectively shape the perceptions of large numbers of people regarding the same things. But oral literature has its own advantages: it is flexible, ambiguous, deniable, adaptable to a range of contexts, and open to many interpretations. A skilled oral poet can expand a tale to last a week or contract it to a few lines of poetry and can use the same tale to praise a king or to lampoon him. Those trained in oral literature have a great capacity to remember, invent, and satirize. While texts, with their efficiency, are useful for states that need to organize masses of people in disparate regions, the assets of verbal performance make it a useful medium for those who feel themselves restricted by states and their texts. Perhaps it is unsurprising that old-time oral storytelling was reviving in this region of China.

As Aye Zai Guang took his friends and me to meet oral poets, we learned about the technical side of the art: the training of singers, the format of changkhap oral poetry (structure, melody, instrumentation, and rhyme schemes), the use of formulaic phrases and

Buddhist arcana, the origins of the form, and its aesthetics. We also learned about the chasm that had emerged between oral storytelling and the textual representations of it in the early stages of the Chinese state. Through a "simplifying project" that aimed to represent ethnic folk culture on the national stage while also "improving" it, the state had dramatically reshaped Tai Lüe oral poetry and dance from the 1950s through the 1980s, creating the "front stage" arena that was now sold to tourists.

Khanan Zhuai, the best-known changkhap poet in Sipsong-panna, had been personally caught up in this process; elevated as a national star under Mao, he had composed praise songs for the Party, including the one quoted above. In the process, the singer and government editors collectively rewrote his songs in Chinese, simplifying them to make them more accessible, and using them to help legitimize a party-state that would rule over ethnic peoples. Gradually, state control of ethnic culture and China's rapid modernization had erased much of his audience, making them illiterate in the old poetic language. In secret, though, Khanan Zhuai had continued singing the older, less politically acceptable songs for a small audience of fans like Aye Zai Guang. His mastery of the older material made him an interesting figure to some younger Tai Lües, and his performance of a fragment of one of these songs sparked a discussion among some of them about their future.

Khanan Zhuai still owned a framed black-and-white photograph of himself laughing with Chairman Mao, which hung in a position of pride on the wooden wall of his stilt house. He was the eagle that flew from Yunnan's rainforests all the way to Beijing, but at eighty-six he looked tired. His shoulders, once broad, now sagged, and the suit jacket he wore over a gray cardigan was dusty at the cuffs. "I am old," he said, "but I don't feel old, my heart feels young." His regal bearing had not diminished, though his audience had shrunk and shifted around him.

Khanan Zhuai's moment on the national stage having passed, he and his wife settled back into their old family stilt house on a back road of Gatsai (Gasa in Chinese). Gatsai is about two miles from Jinghong, located past the new international airport and through a few paddies, and this was where we went to interview him.

Leaving behind the Journey to the East café and making excuses to my Tai Lüe teacher for missing lessons that day, I traveled to interview Khanan Zhuai on a typically warm morning in January. The group accompanying me included Aye Zai Guang, his friend Aye Awn Noy, a Han Chinese colleague who was lending us his company car, and my friend E La. The day was bright and hot, with clear blue skies and no clouds to block the sun. Negotiating the smog, dust, revving motorcycle engines, honking buses, and cries of bus drivers hawking tickets (*Jinghong-ah!*), we turned off the main drag of Gatsai and emerged in a quiet, narrow side street. It was lined with baked white-clay walls, tall trees, and the low walls of stilt-house roofs peering between them. The name Gatsai means "sandy market," and it was historically a market town appended to the city-state, or *muang*, of Jinghong. It was named a separate township during the reorganization of local government that happened post-1953, a separation that still rankles Tai Lües in both places who feel that the old political geography should be kept intact. The big van twisted back and forth through the maze, as Aye Zai Guang and Aye Awn Noy argued about directions.

Aye Awn Noy was twenty years younger than Aye Zai Guang, but they were close friends. Aye Awn Noy did not share Aye Zai Guang's apparently limitless faith in human nature; Aye Awn Noy's cherubic face and oversized glasses hid a wry cynic and, despite his wedding ring, a veteran ladies' man. But beneath the cynicism was another layer of idealism—Aye Awn Noy loved the old ways as much as his older friend and spent most of his waking moments in the villages documenting local folk practices in photographs and videos. He ate dinner with a group of oral poets, including E Guang, almost every week, staying up until the early hours to debate the merits of this or that singer or old tale.

"It's down this way, keep going, keep going," said Aye Zai Guang in Jinghong dialect, his voice hoarse with cigarettes, until we pulled up at a dead end, a whitewashed wall. "This isn't right. Did we take a wrong turn?"

"*Aiyo*," exclaimed Aye Awn Noy. "It can't be possible to get lost in a town as small as Gatsai."

"No problem," said Aye Zai Guang, with a self-deprecating laugh. "We're not lost. It's down the other end." He turned to me and spoke loudly in Chinese. He had a tendency to shout as if he thought I was deaf. "No problem, ga!" he shouted. The van, which barely fit in the narrow alley, made a K-turn into the front yard of a stilt house and nearly hit a rooster. The bird squawked and high-stepped into a bush. "Don't hit the chicken! That's their dinner," Aye Awn Noy said.

The driver, Li Qing, who was lending us his government office's van as a favor (the Chinese rural economy runs on a complex system of personal favors), twisted around and wrestled with the ungainly van's blind spots. A few voluptuous middle-aged women walked by, wearing long, flowered skirts and straw hats and carrying straw baskets that were mostly empty after a successful morning selling their family's produce at the Gatsai market. The van creaked to a halt.

Aye Zai Guang peered out the van's grimy windows: *"Pai, ah?* [Who is that?]"

One of the women peered in the window and said, "Hey, that's Aye Zai Guang, *naw!"* The two women called out in Tai Lüe, inter-rupting each other.

"What are you doing in Gatsai?"

"Oho, he's got a white girl in there!"

"What is he up to with the whitey?"

"No good, I bet, naw!"

"I bet his wife doesn't know about this!"

"Let's go call her, right now." They grinned under their floppy hats. Aye Zai Guang's wife was a government official of higher rank than her husband, making him the subject of endless teasing.

He laughed in embarrassment. "We're going to look for Khanan Zhuai," he answered. "The whitey's going to interview him. Let's meet for lunch later—my treat!"

"Sure!" They fixed a location, and the women shouldered their baskets, with perhaps a little extra swing in their walk for the men from Jinghong.

Aye Awn Noy lit another cigarette, handing one to the driver, who took it in silence. The van navigated a succession of ever-narrowing alleys between the stilt houses and the clean white walls, bumping over rain-made ruts in the dirt road. We wound up at a stilt house at the end of a white-walled dirt path, overlooking a span of rice fields that stretched in pale splendor to a ring of blue mountains. E La, who was along for the day in a blue silk suit as whitey's official translator, murmured, "Great view." Aye Awn Noy coolly draped an arm over her shoulders and she slapped him in annoyance.

Meanwhile, Aye Zai Guang began orchestrating the meeting. He jumped down first, hustled me out of the van and told me to stand and wait, then ran up the ladder of the stilt house, and came back down escorting a smiling, elderly man in a gray suit and a white Tai Lüe head-scarf. At Aye Zai Guang's cue, I wai'ed in the traditional Tai Lüe greeting, Khanan Zhuai bowed back, we shook hands American-style, and took a stiffly-posed photograph in front of his house. Then we climbed up to sit on the porch on miniature wicker stools and drink fresh, powerful tea out of hot glasses. Khanan Zhuai's wife hovered in the doorway, while the rest of us sat crouched around a tape recorder as if it was the machine we were honoring and began the interview.

Since then, the interview and the song Khanan Zhuai sang during it have become texts that I return to often, each time with a slightly different interpretation, to hear something new. The tape is rich, filled with the rustle of our bodies, the sounds of chirping birds sitting in the branches of the tree that hovered in front of the stilt-house porch, of wind in the nearby rice fields, and the sound of someone chopping something in the stilt house next door, the sounds of glasses of tea being picked up and set down on the wooden floorboards near the recorder, and the occasional hoarse croak of a rooster. These sounds recall the heat of the sun baking the porch and transport this listener, at least, back to a morning on which I understood not enough Chinese and no Tai Lüe, less than I can make out now anyway, and so couldn't always follow my own interview. Unintentionally, I wound up echoing one of my teachers, Margaret Mills, who writes of a night of indirectly subversive storytelling by two Afghan performers under the gaze of a representative of the local government. The exchange, she later surmises, might not have taken place had she been a more adept speaker in the local dialect:

My language problems prevented me . . . from verbally asserting a presence which might have distracted the storytellers from the oblique representation of preexisting relationships which so enriched this storytelling session. If I could have distanced myself from the peremptory, systematically antitraditionalist [government official], I would have tried to do so and thus perhaps not have heard the rich but focused discourse addressed to him through Mokhtar and me as his guests.[2]

Mills's narration of her evening in Afghanistan makes an argument for the deep understanding of a performance's context in order to grasp an oral "text."[3] While many oral storytellers, including Tai Lües, write their tales down as text, an oral performance is almost never a static recitation—teller, memorized words, improvised words, and the performative context interrelate and emerge together in a dialectical relationship, as part of a dynamic and creative tradition.[4] In parts of the world where the spoken word is likely to be self-censored for political reasons, context may provide the only clues to meanings below the surface, as with Khanan Zhuai's performance later that morning.

In our interview, the absence of eavesdropping government officials and our location in a stilt house on the edge of town created a relaxed opening for conversation, debate, and song. Our small group included two generations of Tais—Aye Zai Guang and his old colleague and friend, Khanan Zhuai, and the younger Aye Awn Noy and E La. The tape of their conversation, pegged to "my interview," is a braid of overlapping and contrasting voices, dialects, and languages. Khanan Zhuai understood Chinese but would not speak it—like another old socialist poet, Pablo Neruda, he preferred his own language. E La became so interested in what was being said that she often forgot to translate. Also, it turned out that because she was a young woman she was not equipped to translate some of the more classical Tai Lüe turns of phrase. Thus the tape recording is full of conversation between her and the men in the Jinghong dialect, with my anxious voice interjecting questions in stilted, Beijing Chinese learned in U.S. language classes. Aye Zai Guang, Aye Awn Noy, and E La would respond slowly and patiently in their heavily accented and local dialect of Mandarin, repeating themselves if they thought I did not understand them. But as the conversation wore on they omitted more and more. Around and between this exchange, the Tai Lüe–language conversation between Khanan Zhuai and Aye Zai Guang, who had known each other for decades, rippled and flowed, barely audible, sometimes almost murmured.

Because of the song's rarity, this was in many ways the most important song I was allowed to record in Sipsongpanna. Later, in transcribing and translating the interview and the song Khanan Zhuai sang that day, I sought out others to help make sense of the text—monks at the Buddhist temple, elders, friends, various expats who listened to the tape at the Journey to the East café—so that the tape is now an orchestra of audible and inaudible, remembered voices. All these tensions among languages, statuses, and genders of interviewer, interviewed, and commentators mark the texts that scholars produce and bind up the understanding that we have of the words we are trying to hear.

Training a Poet

KHANAN ZHUAI BEGAN the interview by speaking about his training and the basic things he had had to learn about the genre of changkhap. He had mastered a written repertoire first in order to be able to answer sung challenges about specific topics because changkhap performances are structured as duels, with singers competing to display knowledge. Singers also learn to improvise lyrics in response to challenges, putting one another on the spot with elaborate praise that sometimes conceals humorous put-downs. By earning acclaim from their listeners, singers build up their own status and climb a formal hierarchy.

Born in Gatsai, Khanan Zhuai became a Buddhist novice as a young boy and proceeded up the ranks of the monkhood, studying and memorizing the Tai Lüe canon. "I studied all the classics and the Buddhist sutras," he said in Tai Lüe. "If you want to sing, you have to have a wide body of knowledge, especially of Buddhism. There are stories in the Buddhist scriptures, and I [later] took these stories and rewrote them as songs."

At the age of twenty-three, Khanan Zhuai left monastic life, exchanging his monastic title Du for the title given a former senior monk, Khanan, and returned to his family home to farm their fields. While he worked he began studying changkhap song—teaching himself, unusually, without apprenticing himself to any other singers. Most changkhap begin their apprenticeships as adolescents, so he had a lot of ground to cover. "To be a changkhap muang, a poet laureate for the kingdom, you need wide knowledge," he said in Tai Lüe. "You need the knowledge of each place, you need to know praise songs for rulers and for peasants; without all of that, you can't become changkhap muang."

The others interjected, explaining in Chinese. "When you duel with a singer," said E La, "whatever they ask you, you have to be able to answer it. They use lyrics to challenge you."

Aye Awn Noy added, "You study all this material and you master it so you can produce it to explain things, see."

Aye Zai Guang said, slowly and loudly, "For instance! In the wedding ceremony, you must be able to answer and explicate the origins of the wedding ritual. Why is it necessary to slaughter a chicken, why do you have to take down a banana leaf—I'll explain this to you later—the man, the woman, you have to explain these things, ga!"

Aye Zai Guang continued, laboriously: "Another example is the praise ceremony for a new house. You have to explain the origins of the house, the pillars, the beams; you must be able to answer these questions." Similarly, "if you have a monk-initiation ceremony, you have to be able to tell where Sakyamuni [the Buddha] was born, where did he come from, where did he go, what did he preach." He shouted, "It's a lot of things to learn!"

"A singer who can answer all these questions," E La concluded, "will really be approved of by the listeners."

Singers learned to answer questions by memorizing the answers, but part of each performance also involved improvised duels with other singers. So apprentice singers also work on learning to improvise poetry on the spot about any subject—as Tai Lües put it, *han baosang khap baosang* ("see whatever and sing whatever"). This was not easy—in the most common classical rhyme scheme the last word of one eight- to twelve-word line rhymed with the third or fourth word of the next line:

```
X X X X X X X X A
X X A X X X X X B
X X X B X X X X C
X X C X X X X X D
```
and so on.

Most changkhap performances last many hours—usually, all night—so changkhap need a lot of imagery, references, and rhymes at their fingertips in order to be ready to rhyme on any subject.

Khanan Zhuai's first public performance was the epic narration of the "Housewarming Song" (in Tai Lüe, "Heua heuan mai," or "praising the new home") for a house-blessing ceremony, and he remembered being extremely nervous that first time. The performance went well, though, and he spent two years performing by invitation at housewarmings, weddings, and village festivals. Khanan Zhuai's reputation quickly spread, attracting crowds to each performance.

Normally, famous singers jousted at biannual competitions for a position at court. But just two years after he began singing, the "*chao phaendin*" or prince of Sipsongpanna invited Khanan Zhuai to give a command performance.[5] Without any other public competition, the prince named him changkhap muang. Khanan Zhuai moved into Jinghong, was given a title, and took a position at court.

According to historian Quan Quan, a Sipsongpanna Tai Lüe prince formalized these court positions in the mid-fifteenth century, when local cultural flourishing reached its peak.[6] The prince of the day was a patron of the arts, choosing the top oral poets after a public competition and inviting them to live at court. He established four competitive genres and a series of grades for professional and apprentice oral poets, with separate divisions for men and women.[7] The singer who won these competitions was named the changkhap muang, or poet laureate of Sipsongpanna. He had to be someone who could whip the audience into a frenzy with his poetry. If he did it well, he profited. Khanan Zhuai remembered:

> When I used to perform, the host would pay me ten round silver coins, but when I got to the high point of the song, the audience got so

excited, they pulled out whatever coins they had in their pockets and threw them at me—they would explode with coins.

"To the Tai people," Khanan Zhuai remembered, "our changkhap were like the flower of the kingdom. The statesmen loved us, the people loved us, and we were the flowers." No occasion would be complete without a professional singer to praise it: "If you're celebrating and you kill a pig but don't invite a changkhap, then it's like you've killed a pig for nothing because the meat has no taste. You may drink wine, but it is wasted drunkenness. The host has no face because no one praised him."

While changkhap were often hired to praise, they were also expected to satirize. "You need a rich facility with rhyme," said Khanan Zhuai. "An empty coconut in a tree, a coconut that is very high up, knocking around on the palm tree, that makes no milk, I'd take that coconut to satirize a high-up lord or prince who has no use."

Aye Zai Guang said, "For instance, he used an empty snail shell that has no snail in it but that has been elevated and praised by others—he took that empty snail shell to satirize a useless official. Hearing a changkhap sing was like reading the newspaper."

Even as a member of court himself, Khanan Zhuai continued to go into villages by invitation to perform political satires. "You had to be able to sing for the peasants as well as the prince," Aye Zai Guang said. In many genres in China and elsewhere, oral poets have often performed for audiences from a range of social classes. The best among them learn to improvise and adapt to keep different listeners' attentions, combining a variety of registers of speech and styles of performance.

In this context, what makes or breaks oral poets is their approval by serious fans. These aficionados follow performers from show to show, listen closely to the variations in performance and the differences in performers' repertoires, and discuss them later. They socialize with the performers, buy them dinners, drink with them, and trade gossip. Their judgments often determine a singer's status.

No doubt it was such a group of aficionados that had brought Khanan Zhuai's name to the attention of the prince in the first place. Like any other kind of performer, an oral poet attracts fans of great devotion, discrimination, and obsessiveness. In her memoirs, Beijing drumsinger Zhang Cuifeng recalled honing her performance skills by watching the reactions of a prominent aficionado in the audience.[8] To compete in public duels, ascend a hierarchy of singing titles, and become the beneficiaries of a prominent patron in Sipsongpanna, such as a prince, was to rest on a bedrock of such fans. Folklorist Richard Bauman calls displays of competence in verbal arts "an assumption of accountability to an audience for the way in which communication is carried out."[9]

Having been named changkhap muang, Khanan Zhuai began to hone his craft. He traveled to other neighboring royal houses along the Mekong Delta, lived in these places, studied the local genres, and competed with their singers. Cross-border travel was common in those days and the borders were fluid and unmarked. He spent time in nearby northern Laos and Burma's Shan State, even going as far as northern Thailand. To develop as a poet, he said, "You need the wisdom of north, south, east, and west."

While everyone was discussing this, Aye Awn Noy whispered to me to ask Khanan Zhuai to sing for the tape recorder. I did, and Khanan Zhuai demurred, but Aye Awn Noy, Aye Zai Guang, and E La insisted: "Sing for 'Amayligah,' she's going to play it in America." Khanan Zhuai finally agreed under the condition that Aye Zai Guang accompany him on the reed and went into the house, returning with a bag full of bamboo reeds.

Asking about these, I began to learn about changkhap instrumentation and melody. The three men looked over the reeds and admired them, discussing the workmanship of each one. They were long, thin bamboo tubes with seven holes in front and one in back. Bamboo is used for everything in Sipsongpanna, from roofs to kitchen implements to children's slingshots, and it comes in hundreds of varieties. The reeds used to accompany men were fourteen inches long and the women's reeds were eleven inches long. They looked like flutes, except that in the hole of each bamboo tube was a small, thin metal reed with a slit. These bamboo reeds come in all shapes and configurations and are found throughout mainland Southeast Asia and southwest China. In northern Thailand and Laos, for instance, they are bunched together like

14 *Khanan Zhuai sings on the porch of his stilt house.*

a panpipe with the reed in an external mouthpiece, making the instrument called the *khaen* that accompanies the buoyant dancers who sing northern Thai and Lao oral poetry. Aye Awn Noy was insistent that the best reeds for changkhap were made in Meng Hai, his hometown.

Aye Zai Guang chose a reed he liked and started to play a melody that began like a bird call and oscillated along the same range of notes, as Khanan Zhuai cleared his throat a couple of times and began to chant (fig. 14).

The melody blown by the flute around which the singer weaves his lyrics is the basis and yet the least graspable part of changkhap. When I played tapes bought in a public vegetable market from a traveling salesman for foreign listeners at Journey to the East, they always said the music was monotonous. "Does it just pretty much go on like that?" Bex asked politely. Yet monotonous as it was, notating it was not easy because of the way the musician makes the notes twist and fly up and dip as he blows them, and because the speed of the rhythm varies in the accompanist's interchange with the voice of the singer.

I asked Aye Zai Guang about the melodies later, on a sleepy, warm afternoon while Aye Awn Noy, E La, and others played cards in a stilt house. "There are three kinds of melodies," he said. We were strolling along the narrow footpath between waves of rice seedlings in his home village, a path so worn with use that the prints of toes and the soles of feet could be seen pressed into the earth. "The first is The Leaves of a Coconut Palm Tree Blowing in the Wind, what we call *bao gaeng bay*." This slow, gentle, repeating melody uses longer phrases and few changes. "The second is *sakhay bawng sway*, or Drooping Blades of Grass." This had shorter phrases than the first class. "The third tune is *bao long khwang*, the Waves of the Mekong River," he explained. "That *bao long khwang*, naw!" He chopped his hand like a cleaver rhythmically. "It has a melody that goes up and down quickly, like the way that the waves of the Mekong River lap up and down when a little breeze skips across them. That's how it is."

This melody that beat the rhythm of the river, he explained, was the one that Khanan Zhuai used, though sometimes he combined it with Drooping Blades of Grass; in fact, most singers sing something between the latter two melodies. Melodies also varied from one region to the next anyway, Aye Zai Guang observed, so that singers in Da Menglong sang a totally different range of tunes than singers from Meng Han, three hours' drive away. But while there is room for variation by a skilled changkhap, inexperienced or poor singers are immediately obvious because they stumble around and struggle to float on the rhythm of the waves.

As Aye Zai Guang blew the reed, Khanan Zhuai sang his lyrics. This was a short poem, just a sample piece of introductory praise for the prince, something Khanan Zhuai might have sung before launching into a full recitation of a legend or instructive poem for a major occasion. Such introductions and conclusions to the narrative lyrics were where the poet got to strut his stuff, displaying wit and improvisatory skill. "Khanan Zhuai is the only person in Sipsongpanna who can still sing this song," Aye Zai Guang said later.

As it turned out, Khanan Zhuai was also almost the only person who could still understand it. When I played the tape for E La, a week after the interview, she confessed that she could not. The poetry used too much formal language and too many Buddhist allusions. This was a problem to do with Tai Lüe women's traditional education, she said. "When I was a little girl, my mother told me that the reason why Tai women have to sit below men and wait on them is that we can't become monks and get an education in the temple."

This raised a problem: With no way to translate the poetry, what was the point of recording it? Certainly no one back in the United States would be able to translate it. Young Tai Lües like E La that I had met at Journey to the East could speak Chinese, which I could understand, but they had been influenced too much by Chinese culture to have sophisticated Tai Lüe skills and couldn't understand the song. The people who could understand Khanan Zhuai's song were older Tais, Buddhist monks, and youngsters far out in villages mostly untouched by Chinese culture, but these people couldn't speak enough Chinese to explain it to me. I struggled to write the words myself in Tai Lüe script, using the novices' primer from Wat Pajay, but was stumped by the first few words. Tai Lüe has six tones that affect the meanings of spoken words and there are over sixty letters in the alphabet. Even if I lucked into the correct notation, there was no Tai-Chinese dictionary for looking up the words.

Finally, I took my notes in to show to my language teacher. He took one look at the scrawls and frowned, gesturing for the tape. He slapped the tape into his old tape deck, listened to the first few lines, shook his head in disgust over my notations in Tai Lüe, and said, "Just leave me the tape." A few days later he handed me the lyrics written in classical Tai Lüe.

"Next time, bring me a clearer tape," he said tersely. "Khanan Zhuai was a great singer once, but sometimes older people lose their teeth."

We made translating his notation into part of each day's language lessons. Because he too found many of the words obscure, the translation of Khanan Zhuai's short song text became a group project, with a number of monks, elders, and visitors to the temple stepping in and out of the text to offer their interpretations.

The singer began,

"*Chao, heaui chao, heaui . . . heauiii . . . heaui . . .*," or "Prince, hey prince, hey . . . heyyy . . . hey . . ."

Was this line addressed directly to the prince himself? I noticed that on other changkhap tapes bought in street markets the singers used the same line to open their songs. Surely they weren't all performing for the prince.

To answer this and other questions, I invited Aye Awn Noy out for beers. He hemmed and hawed a while and then asked if we could call E La and get her to join us. Once she warily agreed to stop by, he explained that the line had to do with the origins of the genre.

The first changkhap, he said, was a bird that flew into the forest near a village and began to sing. Its song was so beautiful that the whole village came out to listen, including one beautiful girl who spent every day listening for hours. The evil prince of the village, who loved the girl, killed the bird out of jealousy, and it died in her arms. She began to sing back to the bird as it died, imitating its song, and she became the first changkhap. She covered her face with the bird's wing, and since then changkhap singers have always hidden their faces from the audience with fans made of feathers—a style that some poets say helps them to concentrate on the lyrics.

"When a changkhap begins to perform," said Aye Awn Noy, cracking sunflower seeds with his teeth, "he calls out to the spirit of the bird that is watching from above, inviting it to listen in and even, some people say, fly down and inhabit the body of the performer." He grinned and spit out empty seeds onto the ground. "Some singers think that the first changkhap will come down andhelp them remember the words." The "Prince, hey Prince" line was what folklorists such as Milman Parry and Albert Bates Lord, and later Dennis Tedlock, have considered formulaic phrases, often used as pegs on which to hang longer, improvised oral poetry.[10]

Khanan Zhuai continued,

Now, hear my song,
Lady, lovely as a drop of cooking oil,
as dew drops frozen on the ground,
who makes me feel similarly still and peaceful.

Here we had another formulaic phrase: "Now" ("*Ah batdiew wanni,*" literally, "Ah, right now, today") is a formal opening to a new verse. "Now, hear my song, lady," is the opening to a performance.

Changkhap normally perform in male-female pairs, taking turns to continue the narrative performance. A host invites a large group to his or her home, including a couple of professional changkhap—at least one male and one female singer, though sometimes more. Any adult in the room who fancies him- or herself a good singer may start things off with a few lines, an open challenge, usually framed as a love song. A few other singers of the opposite sex may take up this challenge, and all the singers duel verbally. As the audience cheers singers they like and shouts down those they don't, a few top singers emerge and continue the exchange. Eventually a singer challenges one of the professionals hired for the evening to perform a narrative poem for the occasion—a poem about the spiritual significance of Tai Lüe architecture if the festival is a housewarming, or a Buddhist legend if one of the sons of the house has just initiated as a monk.

The singer who has been challenged (and who should have prepared for the performance, as he or she was hired to do this) then embarks on the first chapter of the narrative. However, each chapter is introduced and closed by a few minutes of improvised poetry praising the other singer's attractiveness and wisdom. Some poets, especially but not always women, tend to keep these praise lyrics modest; others, especially men, make the lyrics raunchy and sexually explicit, encouraging the audience to cheer them on. Khanan Zhuai's introductory lyrics praised the imaginary woman singer who would have been his singing partner. "Cooking oil and dew look shiny and beautiful when the light hits them," said the monk, making the comparison a flattering one.

He continued,

Lord Chang See recorded these events for throngs of later
    descendants;
Now I have taken his meritorious deed
And will share it with the world,
Raise it up, align it properly, and split it into parts.

The reference to Lord Chang See was so arcane that none of the monks could explain it except as a possible reference to a long-forgotten author of history texts. The "events" referred to here would have been the historical tale Khanan Zhuai was about to perform for the prince. When he talks about raising the tale up, aligning it, and splitting it into parts, he is making an allusion to tale telling being like house building. Tai Lüe stilt house construction involves raising sacred pillars, the trunks of rainforest trees, to be the frame of the house, and then marking off different sections of the pillars for the ancestral spirits. These spirits inhabit the structure of the stilt house, biding their time to be reborn. In the same way, singers take a long epic inhabited by spirits of people who have passed and divide the epic into serial chapters. Like carpenters, they establish structures that other people enter into.

Then, Khanan Zhuai wove in references to Buddhist mythology that praised the prince by association:

> Now I pray to the Dom Gaun stupa, taking this holy moment to pray,
> Now I open my mouth to speak, drooping [like a leaf on a tree]
> and folding my hands before See Vadan.
> Now, oh, this joyous man whispers "Sa, Sa,"
> folding his hands with a deep and heartfelt reverence.

My monk teacher became preoccupied with the references to Dom Gaun and See Vadan, which he could not identify. He asked around at the temple and heard nothing conclusive until the senior monk who had arranged my lessons in the first place returned from a trip to Thailand. This gentleman, recuperating from his trip with his feet raised, sandals off and a bowl of Thai fruit before him, explained that Dom Gaun was the name of the reliquary in heaven where the gods preserve the hair of the Sakyamuni Buddha. He was dismayed that none of the Wat Pajay monks knew something so basic. "You see what the state is of our traditional education in Sipsongpanna?" he asked me, and sighed.

But what about See Vadan? "It means four fingers," said Aye Zai Guang loudly, as if it were self-evident. "*See* means four, and *vadan* is an old-time word for fingers. He's saying, 'I fold my hands and these four fingers.' Wah, I don't think you should ask that young monk to help you translate—he's too young, he's too influenced by Chinese culture, he'll get it all wrong."

I went back to the monk, who shook his head: "Aye Zai Guang knows a lot, but he's getting old and confused. Four fingers?" He mused for a moment and then looked up, inspired. "You met Khanan Zhuai. Had he lost some fingers in a farming accident?" No, Khanan Zhuai had all ten fingers. "Well, then, that makes no sense."

A month later, the monk went home to visit his family for a holiday and while there he trekked out by foot to see an elderly uncle, a former monk who lived in a distant stilt house. "He knows everything," said the monk. His uncle told him that See Vadan was the name of the first reliquary ever built in Sipsongpanna; it had once stood next to Wat Pajay but had been destroyed. He dictated the names of temples and sacred sites lost during the civil war and Cultural Revolution, and my monk teacher kept the slip of paper with this list in his robes.

"Sa, sa" was easy—even I had heard Tai Lüe laypeople murmur this while throwing rice at monks during Buddhist processions. It may derive from the Indian "*sadhu*," a term for a holy man, spoken over holy sadhus in procession.

The next part of the song showed some mild humor. Changkhap poetry often alternates between the sacred and the profane, mixing classical references and everyday images like these:

The task falls to me, the changkhap,
I may not ask others to take on my duty.
[But if] I make sweet speech bland and tasteless, do not be angry.
I have opened my mouth so wide, hey, and made a lot of noise—
I fear, if I raise my foot to take the next step, I will slip and fall.
I fear you, raising the lid of the pot to eat dinner, have instead gotten
a burst of steam that explodes in your face,
But I blow the steam away and implore you to go on listening,
To stay on with me, as the time drags on.

The image of the song like a bamboo steamer, with hungry diners getting nothing but a face of hot air that the singer cools off by blowing it away, displays the gentle wit of Khanan Zhuai's poetry.

The song continued:

> Now, I have been invited to sing you into the bliss of paradise.
> I [the black-eyed one] fold my hands and pray,
> Please continue your chopping blades,
> You honorable people are all sitting properly, according to
>   the custom,
> Our father, as tall as a Bodawng tree, is bowing humbly as that
>   tree bows.

No one could make sense of this. My teacher simply shook his head. Why the chopping blades—were they imaginary preparations underway for a banquet or a reference to the people actually chopping next door while we sat recording the song? What was a Bodawng tree? The monk thought it might be a kind of bamboo, as it is used as a simile for bowing. Both Tedlock and Jerome Rothenberg have noted the use in oral poetry of terse language and "stripped-down forms that require maximal interpolation by audiences."[11] The problem here was either that the singer had, with age, become confused, or that an audience capable of interpolating these kinds of traditional meanings no longer existed.

In the concluding section, Khanan Zhuai wove a complex metaphor and pointed to a climax:

> Now, that which shimmers white like your clothes,
> Each one perfectly formed, guarding an inner treasure [like]
>   a monastery,
> That which we raise over our heads with both hands is a plate
>   full of popped rice.
> We raise it high, over our worthless hearts,
> as high as our noses and mouths:
> Who will we use this to honor?

Tai Lües traditionally wear white clothes to go to temples on major holidays. Here they "guard an inner treasure," the pious heart, in the same way that the monastery preserves the treasure of Buddhist wisdom inside it. All these images—the white clothes of the people enclosing pure hearts, the monastery enclosing the treasure of Buddhist knowledge—are used to enhance the image of white popped rice with its golden kernels. Tai Lües throw popped rice at honorees at major ceremonies, and they raise it high as a sign of respect—the higher the position relative to the face, the higher the level of respect. The litany of images concludes with a rhetorical question: Whom are we honoring? The answer is the prince, who encloses honor and treasure as do all these other images. "This is pretty good. You can see here that he used to be a very good poet," said the monk.

> Now, the ten great lords and ten high noblemen entering, and
>   the twenty courtiers who are already arrived, who have they come
>   to honor?
> Ah, now,
> I whisper "sa, sa" with great joy, I throw myself on the ground and
>   go on praying
> But I, the changkhap, should learn a little humility, and stop here.

As he finished the song, Khanan Zhuai coughed again. "That was no good," he concluded. "When I was young, I could sing till I was red in the face. Now I sing poorly." This was modest; he was the only person living who could sing this song at all. The reasons for this had as much to do with modernization as with the process of reshaping minority culture undertaken by the state that began in the 1950s. The irony is that Khanan Zhuai was at the center of the state's editing and rewriting of Tai Lüe identity during that period; his appropriated poetry was part of the simplifying process that eventually drove his own oral literature underground and erased much of his audience.

China Reconstructs

IN THE FALL 1953 issue of an official Chinese magazine aimed at foreign readers, Chen Hanseng describes the backdrop to Khan-an Zhuai's most famous performance. It took place at a gathering of 10,000 people along the banks of the Mekong to "celebrate the establishment of the Thai Autonomous Region," a newly formed department of the four-year-old People's Republic of China. The crowds were huge and the celebrants "proud of their nationality. Their delegates too would participate in the newly organized government."[12] Chen paints a picture of the exuberant celebration:

> In a dozen Buddhist temples the monks offered prayers for the happiness and prosperity of the autonomous region. On the river, the young men held dragon-boat races. On the shore, the elephants paraded. Singing and dancing and lantern slide shows went on until after midnight. Never before had [Jinghong] enjoyed such a holiday.[13]

Khanan Zhuai was in his late thirties and at the height of his career. Like many Tai Lües, he had participated in the war against Japan and the war against the Kuomintang that led to the Communist triumph. Now he was welcoming the establishment of a new nation, which in turn raised him up as an icon of pan-ethnic national unity.

As Chen describes, Tai Lües in Sipsongpanna had suffered and had paid exorbitant taxes while under the rule of Chiang Kai-shek. They watched their silver resources dribble away as they became increasingly dependent on imports from Kunming, and their economy disintegrated under a monopoly system of tea plantations run by the Chiang regime. Some Tai Lüe nobles, including Zhao Cun Xin, the last prince of Jinghong, joined the Chinese Communist Party and fought for the establishment of the new nation. When the People's Liberation Army won, some Tai Lüe elites, like Mr. Dao, were appointed to high-ranking positions in the new local government. Those who opposed the new government generally voted with their feet and moved across the borders.

To celebrate the "liberation" of Sipsongpanna, Khanan Zhuai composed and performed a song welcoming the Beijing delegation. The poem became his signature song and he sang it again in Beijing for Mao. He was flown up to Beijing five times altogether to sing for Mao Zedong and Zhou Enlai. Khanan Zhuai and Aye Zai Guang were both appointed to local cultural committees. This poem was translated into Chinese, edited, and published in a popular collection of Khanan Zhuai's poetry, *Dai jiaren zhi ge* (Songs of the Dai family).

His poetry became an emblem of the socialist state's harmonious relationships with ethnic minorities. But in the process, the poetry had begun to change.

This poem begins, not with an invocation to the spirit of the first changkhap, but with an invocation of the newly-invented Chinese "Dai" ethnic group, a miniature "imagined community" within the borders of the nation-state:

> O Listen, Dai family, O,
> O please quietly listen,
> I shall sing of our nationality,
> How we crossed over from hell into paradise.

Drawing from Tai Lüe legends about their original migration to Sipsongpanna, the poem charts how the migrants found their home on the banks of the Mekong River. These people, he told, built a kingdom ruled by cruel feudalism, which "coiled up around the forest like a poisonous snake." This sentiment was in striking contrast to his songs in Tai Lüe of praise for the prince who had named him changkhap muang.

As Khanan Zhuai recounted in this poem, Tai Lües were liberated when the sun, a Chinese symbol of Mao Zedong, arose in Beijing and warmed the forest, bringing it new life:

> O Listen! My brothers,
> In the midnight of our Dai family's suffering,
> The sun rose in Beijing, heart of our ancestral homeland,
> The warm sun shone deep into the heart of the Lancang River,
> The lacquer-black forest was transformed into a shining pavilion,
> Colored clouds rose into the air above the Bodhi tree,
> The white elephant emerged from the forest,
> The phoenix flew up and basked in the sunlight,
> A thousand lotus petals opened on the ground,
> And gongs and elephant's foot drums beat the rhythm of the river.

In many respects the Chinese poem is a kind of faux oral poem, incorporating frequent "Os" and "Ahs" and "Listen, Tai brothers" that sound the way someone might imagine ethnic minority oral poetry to sound if they had never actually listened to it.[14] But this poem omits the unique elements that really are formulaic phrases in Tai Lüe oral poetry, lines like "Prince, hey Prince." This praise song for the Party also handles religion very differently than the praise song for the prince that Khanan Zhuai performed for us. This one welds some basic, universal Buddhist iconography—the sacred Bodhi tree, the good omen of the white elephant, the thousand lotus petals—onto Maoist iconography—the sun rising in Beijing. He omits any complicated or tricky Theravada Buddhist references to reliquaries or dead Tai Lüe historians that Mahayana Buddhist Chinese readers might not grasp. He adds in a litany of vivid symbols of Sipsongpanna: the drums, birds, river, and forest pile on each other, a list of offerings to Beijing. "I wrote that poem," he said in our interview, "because I really did believe that things were better. At that time, everyone seemed happier."

Like the poet himself, Khanan Zhuai's very local and specific poetry had been caught up in the much larger and general production of a national imagined community in which ethnic minorities were to play a limited and supporting role. This simplifying project was the culmination of the grassroots May Fourth Movement that had aimed to excavate and raise up vernacular and folk culture and that had begun thirty years earlier. Through a process of appropriation, editing, and reinvention, oral literature that had represented high, elite culture in the princedom of Sipsongpanna would become low, folk culture in the context of a larger nation-state.

The process continued, appropriating ethnic performance traditions, reshaping them, and either eliminating elements that did not fit the new, simpler, nationalized model, or driving them underground. The simpler and more manageable ethnic tropes, eventually separated from the authors who created them, were then, and are still, used by state-controlled media to mark and incorporate unstable national borders.

"O, cousins from Beijing!" the poem concludes:

You bring light and hope into Tai family villages,
The forest fills with the rising sound of our grateful song.

Ethnic oral poets like Khanan Zhuai authored many of China's most powerful and enticing folk images, some of which live on today in the front stage of mass tourism.

The Simplifying Project: Folktales

WHILE LANGUAGE COMMITTEES simplified ethnic alphabets and languages, culture committees simplified their oral poetry in edited volumes of ethnic folklore. Dozens of these volumes, such as *The Seven Sisters: Collected Chinese Folk Stories*, were produced (and are still produced today), and they share a number of commonalities.[15]

First, the folktales in these collections were presented as authorless. They were presented not as the creations of individual tellers, such as Khanan Zhuai, who might put their own spin or interpretation on the tales for princes or peasants. Rather, they were presented as essential, idealized texts produced by a homogeneous group that spoke with one voice. This lack of authorship unified the group that the tales are intended to represent, while at the same time suggesting a lack of ability by members of the group to think critically or individually. As Hung Chang-tai observes, this view was much like that of the Grimm Brothers during their romantic nineteenth-century efforts to collect tales that established a German national folk culture.[16] One 1920s Chinese folklorist wrote:

Folk literature . . . is produced by a community and not by individuals. Generally, literary works are works of individual authors . . . but this is not the case with folk literature. It is not produced by a particular writer or artist. Rather, it is the product of an entire community.[17]

Of course, this is not true of oral literature, especially those genres in which performers compete to write and improvise complex lyrics. That kind of complexity, however, does not fit into the political views that sometimes underlie collections of folklore.

The tales in these folklore collections also tend to be simple, even childlike in style and language. They are published in the national vernacular, usually without passing through an intermediate stage of recording and notating in the original language. Thus complexities of repetition, allusion, and indirection are edited out at an early stage, as are references to specific places or times; this places the folk group in an eternal present. References to texts and to religious literature are omitted. There are no puns or wordplay. The tales are cleansed of the sexual joking that characterizes Tai Lüe oral poetry, and the adult flirtation is replaced with innocent romanticism. In effect, this infantilizes the collective that the songs are said to represent, bringing them down to a manageable stature.

The tales or discussions of them also often emphasize an ethnic intimacy with nature. For instance, the *Simple History of the Dai Nationality* refers to a Tai legend in which an ancestor marries several women who are part-tiger as evidence of the "chaotic" nature of Tai Lüe marriage practices.[18]

Finally, the politics of the tales are nationalized. Poems that may have originally ironically satirized local nobility, as Khanan Zhuai and his fans pointed out, were now replaced by unambiguous praise for the Party; editors of folktale collections could thus claim that the tales "reflect the pursuit of an ideal society and happiness of the Dai people."[19] References to other places in mainland Southeast Asia, with which Tai Lüe oral poets such as Khanan Zhuai had close and regular contact, were often omitted to emphasize the containment of Tai Lües within Chinese borders. Where there was mention of a location outside of Sipsongpanna, that location was always Beijing, the nation's capital. Such texts reoriented border-crossing minorities such as the Tai Lüe toward their new center and emphasized their containment within the borders.

Collectively, these tales served as instructional tools for the discipline of minorities, teaching them what kind of ethnic culture would be permissible in the public realm and what would not. They also taught other Chinese readers, people browsing through bookstores all over Yunnan and the rest of China. All Chinese readers of these books were wound into the national narrative in the vernacular language that joined center with periphery. The edited collections often placed a Han story alongside stories by Hui, Mongol, Miao, Zhuang, Tibetan, and other ethnic groups. All the tales were made equally free of local history, local language, ethnic religion, or local specificities. All minority groups were implicitly as united in the nation as in the pages of the book. The texts had created, as Benedict Anderson put it in another context, a "new way of linking fraternity, power and time meaningfully together" in the nation.[20]

Moreover, the tales become part of foreign policy. The *Seven Sisters* series and others like it were published in English; Chinese ethnic folktale books also teach international audiences how to think about Chinese ethnic groups. In the early 1990s, an American scholar, Lucien Miller, compiled his own lively English translations from similar collections of folktales and saw "almost no evidence of abstract or analytical thinking, definitions, or syllogisms in the stories, all of which are found in literate cultures and are facilitated through the use of written texts."[21] Because the tales derived from oral traditions, he concluded, they "embody a simple, dualistic vision of reality that is distant and distinctive from the complicated ambiguity found in literate culture."[22]

Miller did not, unfortunately, examine the process by which the tales had been collected before he translated them. The "simple, dualistic vision of reality" was more likely that of the editorial collectives publishing the tales than that of the people who told them. Ethnic abstract and analytical thinking, definitions, and syllogisms had been edited out—in effect driven underground. A similar process created the legendary Tai Lüe "peacock dance."

The Simplifying Project: Dance

FROM THE 1950S to the early 1960s, groups of culture bureau workers also engaged in a related project to collect, document, and improve upon other forms of ethnic folk performance besides oral narrative. One such group, led by choreographer Chin Ming, traveled from Beijing to the borderlands of Yunnan to conduct field research and "spent a happy month with the Tai people." There they "fell under the spell of the subtropical scene" and were entranced by a ritual dance that they saw while listening "to the light rustle of the breeze in the coconut palms" and "the muted boom of distant 'elephant leg' drums."[23]

This dance, which is probably related to a Shan ritual *kinnaree* dance still seen across the borders in northern Burma, is traditionally performed by an elder wearing a bird mask made of papier-mâché, wings on his arms, and a long train like a peacock's tail. That it was performed by a man makes sense to anyone who observes peacocks in nature; as my monk teacher observed, "The male peacocks are the colorful ones who display their feathers" as part of mating patterns. The kinnaree dance was performed at a slow and stately pace at Buddhist temple festivals.

Chin Ming wrote that with some creative thinking he and his colleagues were able to improve on this ritual dance:

> Our idea was to make it a group dance for girls so as to intensify the glory of the peacock in a resplendent scene. If the clumsy accessories were discarded, we decided, more emphasis could be laid on a portrayal of the spirit of the bird. . . . Without the mask there could be facial expression, and without the wings there would be much greater freedom of movement.[24]

Once shorn of these distracting elements and of its Buddhist context, the feminized and dramatized *kongque wu* ("peacock dance"), later popularized by the famous Tai Lüe dancer Dao Meilan, became renowned all over China. It became a staple of the prefectural and provincial song-and-dance troupes, and it is performed in hotels and dinner halls in Kunming and Sipsongpanna.

As a result of the dance fad, the peacock has become nationally synonymous with the similarly exotic, colorful, and elegant Tai Lües of Sipsongpanna: "it is the animal most beloved by the Dai nationality," people often say. The peacock is a ubiquitous symbol in the tourism industry, painted onto the buildings of the international airport and the sides of tour buses, and printed on brochures and T-shirts. A touropop CD with the song "Xishuangbanna, My Hometown" features a picture of a beaming dancer in a peacock dress. In several villages I saw young Tai Lüe girls teaching this state-concocted ballet to each other as "our traditional Tai folk dance."

I asked Aye Zai Guang about the peacock. "The peacock is not our symbol," he said emphatically. "It was chosen for us by others. If we had to have an animal to symbolize us, it would be the elephant because that was what we used to ride into warfare." Other Tai Lües expressed similar views. Perhaps a warlike elephant is a more potent and dangerous symbol to choose to stand for the borderlands than a pretty and feminine bird.

As the simplifying project proceeded, other ballets and operas were edited also. One, named after its hero, Prince Sudun ("Chao Sudun"), is based on an episode in one of Sipsongpanna's oral-narrative epic poems, "The Ten-Headed King." Some scholars believe the tale derives from the "Ramayana," an Indian epic narrative. During the 1950s, the tale called "Prince Sudun" was cleansed of any religious or ritual meaning and rewritten as a socialist fable. An opera based on the fable was banned during the Cultural Revolution but now has been revived as a tourist show, performed daily for visitors at Jinghong's Chunhuan Park.

* * *

THE SIMPLIFYING PROJECT reinvented folktales, folk dances, ethnic dress, and even local scripts; it changed the Tai Lüe and other ethnic minorities from peoples with complex oral and written traditions into simple and romantic "folk," and ultimately into silenced and commodified spectacles—feminine bodies on display. Comparing Khanan Zhuai's praise poem for the Party with a song like "Xishuangbanna, My Hometown" shows how much the touropop song draws from the simplified ethnic poem. The litany of images Khanan Zhuai offered to the new patrons in Beijing—listing a treasure trove of colorful birds, happy singing minorities, tropical fruit, and lush rainforests—became emblematic on a national scale of the docility, generosity, and exoticism of southwestern border peoples. His poetry disciplined the borders in the imaginations of those that read and heard it, bringing the complex, unstable new national borders down to a manageable size.

As Anderson tells us, an empire is organized around a high civilization, one with an elite culture and a sacred text. But for those ethnically and linguistically distinct peoples who are incorporated into the new state, the reimagining of the nation as a horizontal comradeship described in shared texts does not result in greater equality but instead in greater marginalization from the dominant group who speak another language.

From the perspective of the working artist, there is nothing contradictory about singing praise for anyone who will throw coins at him. Like a tree, the working artist grows toward the light. But as it turned out, Khanan Zhuai had chosen a fickle patron. In some ways his poetry made the poet himself redundant: he was discarded once the work of establishing the state and its cultural borders was complete. During the Cultural Revolution Khanan Zhuai and other folk performers who had been elevated as model minorities were humiliated and persecuted. One rival poet, Khanan Ying, burned all his lyric sheets in the stove in his home around which he used to perform for village crowds. He died after a harsh period in a labor camp. Others committed suicide or were so psychologically broken that they were never able to sing again. Because he owned a piece of farmland, Khanan Zhuai was denounced as a landlord and sent to the mountains to do labor. He was the only one of his professional peers to survive this period, and he survived surrounded by an audience no longer able to appreciate his craft.

✳ ✳ ✳

A MONTH BEFORE the interview with Khanan Zhuai, Aye Nawn and Aye Soong had held that first Tai Lüe pop concert in Gatsai. It had drawn thousands of young Tai Lües to the town to hear new pop songs and featured a few younger female changkhap including E Guang and E Awn Noy. As we wound up the interview, I asked Khanan Zhuai what he thought about these contemporary changkhap—many of whom later told me that if the prince were still around, he or she would be the changkhap muang. This sparked a lively exchange in Tai Lüe.

Khanan Zhuai gestured down the street—the whole concert had been visible from the porch of his house. He shook his head and said that he liked the contemporary singers personally but that he had a low opinion of their poetry: "Today's singers don't know the Tai Lüe language," he said in Tai Lüe.

Aye Zai Guang and Aye Awn Noy began to chuckle—this was pretty harsh criticism.

Khanan Zhuai continued in Tai Lüe, mentioning E Guang and another popular female changkhap: "They came and sang here but I couldn't understand a word. They may know Tai Lüe but they don't know Tai Lüe songs. They're not the Tai Lüe race—I don't know what race they're supposed to be."

Aye Zai Guang laughed and agreed. The younger pop singers were influenced by Burmese Shan and northern Thai pop songs and borrowed some of their turns of phrase because that was "cool." Older Tai Lües like Aye Zai Guang saw the borrowing as politically subversive and as an abandonment of local traditions, and he said so.

Aye Awn Noy, who was close to the younger changkhap and the pop-song activists, turned to me and translated for me diplomatically in Chinese, "Khanan Zhuai says that he likes the new singers, but that older people have difficulty understanding the words."

"Ah," I said, confused. Clearly more had been said, but translation had been abandoned. Everyone began to pile into the conversation in Tai Lüe with his or her own opinions. Aye Awn Noy was in favor of the younger female singers because he thought they were revitalizing an indigenous cultural form. E La dismissed all the Tai Lüe activism in favor of assimilation into the Chinese mainstream—she loved to listen to the old songs but thought reviving them was a waste of time that would only lead to trouble with the government.

Finally, Khanan Zhuai summed it up, borrowing a Chinese idiom but saying it in Tai Lüe: "Singing for youth today is *si ting heua ho khuai* ['strumming a lute for the ears of a water buffalo']." The others all laughed at the insult.

"To write my poems," Khanan Zhuai remembered, "I listened to everything." He continued: "I would go into the rainforest and sit for hours to listen to the trees and the birds that live on different branches of the trees. I used the sounds of different birds to convey human emotions. For instance, the cry of the cuckoo, *gu? gu! gu? gu!*, is heartbreaking, and I use it to stand for human suffering." Nowadays, he added to Aye Zai Guang, they cannot do this kind of thing anymore because the rainforest is gone.

***

WE BOWED AND said farewell to Khanan Zhuai, who invited us to call him if we had more questions. At a long Tai Lüe luncheon at a friend's café in Gatsai we downed steamed bamboo, fried ferns, chicken livers, and sticky rice, with many shots of rice liquor. After some long, joking exchanges with the village women and more Tai Lüe debate about culture and ethnic identity, we climbed into the van and drove back to Jinghong in silence, drowsy with food and wine. Aye Zai Guang woke up once, confused, and tried to get out of the van while it was still moving. E La and Aye Awn Noy pulled him back in, swearing. The streets were hot and empty after lunch—as the temperature rose over thirty, Sipsongpanna residents were taking longer midday *xiuxi*, or siestas. A few trucks trundled past on the road that lay across the rice fields like an arrow pointing at Jinghong, kicking up clouds as they went.

The airport road was lined with Tai Lüe stilt-house restaurants, all empty now. In one, a woman in a long red skirt stood heavily and leaned over to switch on a crooked, pink standing fan. The sleepiness of the midday road prefigured the quiet that would descend on it when the big superhighway from the airport was finished and this old road past the airport became obsolete, and the exhausted silence that would settle a few years later, when Jinghong's tourism economy abruptly bottomed out. As we trundled into the center of town, along broad new roads lined with silent noontime hotels, we passed a row of white tour buses sitting under the hotels' drooping red and blue opening banners. A bus driver dozed in each driver's seat, arms folded, legs propped up, with baseball caps pulled over the eyes. The sides of the buses were emblazoned with the worn and dusty images of peacocks.

O Chairman Mao's Communist Party!
Under your instruction,
We are determined to use our own hands,
and on this land soaked with our own blood
we will build a joyous paradise.[25]

4

The Monks

The weather was growing hotter, and with each passing
day the temperature crept further past forty. One day, as
I went for a morning jog around the hotel compound,
I noticed a Chinese man, a tourist in a yellow baseball cap, hiding
behind a tree and photographing the jogging foreign woman. To
escape the tourists, I moved out of the government guesthouse and
into the home of a German botanist, where I rented a room on the
ground floor. There, after morning Tai Lüe classes and lunch with
Mat at Journey to the East, I crept into a cool, tiled bedroom to study
Chinese texts, doze through the midday tropical heat, and dream, as
clouds of insects descended on the house.

Resembling ants with oversize wings, these insects crawled over
the house's white tiled floor by day and died overnight. Their corpses
blew away by morning, leaving behind only scattered papery wings.
Luscious yellow and pink flowers opened along the streets, with
large nodding heads and protruding red tongues. When I sat on the
small balcony to write daily field notes, huge, technicolor butterflies
flapped lazily up into the air above the balcony railing, then sank
below it and fluttered off. Spring had come to Jinghong.

The arrival of spring meant that the annual Songkran holiday
(called "Water-splashing festival" in Chinese), when throngs of tourists descended on Jinghong, was only weeks away. The monsoon, or
rainy season, would follow and with it a three-month period called
Vasaa. During *Vasaa*, monks went into retreat, devout Buddhists

took special vows and spent more time at the temple, and all public performances—including changkhap—were halted. At about that time my research visa would expire and it would be time to leave Sipsongpanna for good.

Most field research projects, whether they last a week or a year, encounter a dark moment about two-thirds of the way through when the researcher lies down on her bed, looks up at the ceiling, and becomes completely convinced that the project is doomed. This moment can signal one of two possibilities. It can mean that the ethnographer is, in fact, sinking deeper below the surface, adjusting to a subterranean world of secret alliances and multiple meanings, and putting down roots in a deeper substratum of personal networks, perhaps even on the verge of some breakthrough. However, the dark moment can also mean that the research project is actually failing. It is often not possible to know for sure which it was until after the project is over.

From the perspective of those long, hot Jinghong afternoons, progress seemed slow. I biked to the temple every day for Tai Lüe–language lessons, and Aye Zai Guang invited me out almost every night for long meals and epic drinking bouts with his friends and colleagues, dinners where tales were traded, political alliances forged, and business deals brokered in Tai and in Yunnanese. He took a group of us into the villages with him on most weekends for more of the same: long, formal banquets with elderly Tai Lüe men in stilt houses. As the foreign visitor, I was always placed on display in the seat of honor where I sat trapped while Tai Lüe conversation—too advanced for me—was swapped around the table for hours. For months, I sat at Aye Zai Guang's left hand, and we ate our way through mountains of Tai Lüe delicacies in homes and cafes around the prefecture: plates of spicy snails, deep-fried buffalo rinds, barbecued duck fetuses, raw organ meats, raw blood salsa, and fried mountain weeds. These had to be downed with *lao* (a chili-flavored grain liquor) and robust cheers of "*Dok-dok—shay!*"

At times, the hospitality seemed almost menacingly passive-aggressive: if I tried to decline the night's fifth or sixth toast of grain alcohol, the man proposing the toast would ask, "You despise us ethnic minorities, don't you?" Aye Zai Guang would then apologize on my behalf and with great ceremony place large chunks of, for instance, rubbery raw intestine in my bowl, watching closely to make sure I ate it all. Like a child trapped at a table full of adults, I was sometimes instructed to trot out a few words of Tai Lüe, to write my name in Tai, to toast the host in Tai, or to dress up in frilly, lavender-colored Tai Lüe dresses and pose for group photographs. I complied: I had already alienated one major informant in E Guang and could not afford to burn more bridges. But the singers' cancelled appointments and elaborate excuses had by now become clear signals. No more interviews with singers followed that first meeting with Khanan Zhuai.

Meanwhile, Tai Lüe Buddhism was growing below the surface, and the ethnic revival was gradually entering a new stage of political sophistication and clout. As part of this religious resurgence, Tai Lües were reviving old forms of performance. Feasts during Buddhist holidays, like the ones Aye Zai Guang attended and sometimes hosted, were places for political alliance-building and lobbying between Tai Lüe villagers and officials. Within this revival of traditional holidays and celebrations, women and men were occupying new and nontraditional roles as well. As Songkran approached with *Vasaa* on its heels, the number of auspicious dates for holding ceremonies diminished, and so villagers around the prefecture began to increase their activity in back alleys and small towns.

The monks at Wat Pajay, my teacher and his supervisors, were now in constant motion. They went daily to villages to officiate at one or another Buddhist ritual—the initiation of novices, the promotion of novices to the monkhood, the opening of a newly renovated temple, or a monthly full-moon festival—and they began to invite me along. This grassroots movement, inchoate and fluid, seemed to be developing a clearer sense of identity, and it was spilling across the borders; Tai Lües from Laos and Burma were beginning to show up in quantity at ceremonies in Sipsongpanna.

Almost daily, one of the monks would go around gathering up senior monks to officiate at a village ceremony. The monks would gather around the temple's white pickup truck, and anyone who happened to be in the temple courtyard and who had relatives or business along the way, or who just felt like a change of scene, was welcome to jump in the back of the truck. The monks always sat relaxed in front while laypeople, some of them elderly, gripped onto one another's sleeves and bounced off the sides of the truck bed as it leapt on the unpaved back-country roads. The elder villagers wouldn't have had it any other way—the monks were Sipsongpanna's treasures and they had to be taken care of.

A few hours later, the truck would roll into a village humming with preparations. Stilt houses were blasting the whirling flute-sounds of changkhap or the latest Aye Sam songs from their tinny stereos and a few Tai Lüe men, frowning under felt hats and wielding glinting machetes, chased a buffalo, tied skittering to a tree and rolling its eyes in terror. Women in long skirts with their hair in buns ran barefoot up and down the stilt-house ladders carrying metal bowls of rice and shouting instructions for the feast preparations.

On one occasion E La and Aye Awn Noy came along to see a group of eight-year-olds initiate as novices, and we arrived in the temple truck to find the whole village amassed in the square to watch the ceremony. The villagers were leaning from the stilt-house porches, hanging from trees, and peering over one another's shoulders at a group of little boys with shaved heads who shifted anxiously from one foot to the other in their underpants. The village women lined them up in front of an impromptu metal gutter on sticks and took turns dumping metal cups of holy water onto the gutter so that the water splashed the shivering, huddled boys. Then, older relatives dressed the boys, blessed them, and tied white string on their wrists to lock their spirits into their bodies during the transition (fig. 15). Their uncles drove the boys off to the village temple on a pack of motorcycles.

That night, their parents sat the boys up on stacks of mattresses, and family members bowed to the children on their hands and knees. Then the feasting began, and changkhap were brought into the houses to sing until dawn, while dozens of guests ate and drank from low wicker tables and cheered themselves hoarse. The next day, all the village residents marched in procession to the temple carrying money, monks' robes, towels, soap, even driving pigs and cows before them, whatever they had. In the culminating moment, senior monks from Wat Pajay taught the tired boys how to fold, put on, and tie their new robes (fig. 16).

15 A girl watches village boys initiate as Buddhist novices, near Da Menglong.

16 *Senior monks dress new novices in their new robes, near Da Menglong.*

When I returned to Wat Pajay and told my monk teacher about what we had seen, he shook his head in surprise: "When I was promoted to the novitiate we did it very quietly in our living room. It wasn't anything like that." But that had been in the early 1980s, only a few years after the Cultural Revolution. Fifteen years later, Sipsongpanna's Buddhist revival had emerged from the shadows into the village square. The entire ritual would be ordered to a halt while Aye Awn Noy or anyone with a camera was pulled into the middle of the ceremony to document it. "They're afraid the rules will change again and they want to be sure to record these customs for the future," Aye Awn Noy explained.

For now, the threat seemed remote. There seemed no end to the hundreds of Tai Lüe boys ready to initiate and enter temple schools.

* * *

MEANWHILE, TO PROTECT the sensitive feelings of my Tai Lüe colleagues, and in an increasingly desperate effort to break through social barriers and build the trust that might lead to more interviews with singers, I began to endanger my health. Most visitors to Sipsongpanna get stomach ailments, but after months of these I no longer noticed when one ailment ended and another began. Food poisoning, alcohol poisoning, the flu, and amoebic dysentery followed one another, until one day I began to turn yellow.

Hepatitis is one of the most common illnesses in China, but the doctors in Jinghong's new hospital were apparently not equipped to recognize it. China had laid its claim to ethnic border areas like Sipsongpanna with promises of electricity, good schooling, and modern medicine, but as the Maoist state disintegrated and hospitals were forced to privatize most services the country's medical system was collapsing. Inside Jinghong's shiny, brand-new hospital, the scene was as chaotic as any inner-city clinic in the United States. Frightened, red-cheeked women holding squalling babies in elaborately embroidered baby carriers, farmers kneading their dusty black fedoras in battered hands, and men patiently dripping blood from head wounds, all crowded together into the consultation room. The crowd listened in fascination as an inept and harried doctor brushed off the foreigner without looking up from her desk. "You have a head cold—go home and rest," she snapped.

I did, but the botanist in whose home I was staying took a graver view. "If you don't begin to gain weight soon, I will insist that you fly to Beijing to be seen by a real doctor," he said. I agreed but struck a bargain: just wait one more month, until after Songkran, when the rains come. Maybe a break in the tropical heat would bring a research breakthrough, too.

***

"*AIYO*," SAID MY teacher in his room, rubbing his head. "Why do they want to build another temple? Sipsongpanna has so many temples, we can't manage them all." Over 500 temples had been refurbished—torn down and rebuilt from the ground up or built from scratch where an old one used to stand. Now the government theme park wanted to open another one for tourists, and Wat Pajay was objecting. My teacher kept canceling our language classes to go to temple openings or temple meetings in one town or another. They were refurbishing Wat Pajay too, building another hall and a new gate to wall the temple off from the theme park. When I arrived for classes in the mornings, my stocky teacher was often found standing with a hoe in hand, dusty robes hiked up, mixing concrete, while other monks clambered on bamboo scaffolding. "We're making sand castles," he said. "We'll see if they fall down."

Tai Lües in Sipsongpanna, including the monks at Wat Pajay, were not equally happy with all new Buddhist temples. For instance, the Tai Lüe temple built in Kunming as part of a theme park, the Nationalities Villages, came in for special criticism. Like the theme park in Jinghong, but on a larger and more elaborate scale, each of the model villages in this popular park contains small houses, musical and dance displays, souvenir shops, and restaurants. The "Dai mountain hamlet" also has a Buddhist temple and reliquary that are among the park's most popular features. Intriguingly, though, the temple architecture is more like that of a Sipsongpanna Tai Lüe stilt house than that of a Tai Lüe temple, and its internal front-and-center layout is more characteristic of Chinese Mahayana Buddhist spaces than of Tai Lüe temple halls. Its interior is decorated with photographs of the Thai monks who had blessed the temple, and novice monks sit inside, selling incense, all of which give the space an air of authenticity. But Tai Lüe monks in Jinghong called the temple "fake" and said the novices in it were "fake monks." When I asked my monk teacher what that meant, he answered heatedly, "What do you call it when someone puts on the robes and doesn't follow the vows? Fake monks!" Tai Lüe monks also said there were no Buddhist relics in the theme park reliquary. Obviously, there is also no Tai Lüe community around the temple to use it for rituals.

Instead, Sipsongpanna residents were building their own, local temples, and community involvement in these was intense. Elders banded together in village teams to raise the funds for the new buildings, posting lists in old Tai Lüe script detailing how much each family had given. Wat Pajay monks who had studied temple architecture in Thailand were brought in to oversee construction. The new temples were blessed with festivals, including concerts of Tai Lüe song.

17 Monks in procession past Jinghong hotels. The Chinese banner on the lamppost reads: "The people love the people's army."

The villagers' pride in their sons and in the reviving religion demanded even more public recognition. On the January anniversary of China's announcement that it would allow freedom of religion, the monks at Wat Pajay took one of the smaller images of the Buddha out of the temple, put it on the back of a pickup truck, and hooked up a loudspeaker that played tape recordings of monks chanting sutras. The procession gathered at a road where the city was building new hotels (fig 17). About forty senior monks, newly promoted novice students, and their parents and sisters stood in rows. As the truck led the way, the procession wound quietly through downtown Jinghong just as many people were going to work. They marched past taxis and black government cars, past rows of water buffalo being led off to market, past sputtering tractors, and past a few groups of tourists wearing matching red baseball caps who stopped in their tracks and took photographs.

The procession turned into Manting Road, and the dancers and sex workers in Tai Lüe dress sitting on chairs in front of dining halls and brothels got up to watch the procession go by. A few backpackers stepped out of Journey to the East with Anulan and others to take photos. Tai Lües from the villages behind Manting Road's hotels slowly merged into the crowds. A few of the villagers had bowls of popped rice, which they threw at the monks. Some older women kneeled and prayed on the street corners before the monks.

As the procession approached the turnoff from Manting Road to the dirt path to Wat Pajay, all these people—elderly women, dancers, farmers, and tourists—began to fall in behind the monks, slowly, at first cautiously, then with growing ease and cheerfulness. It was turning into a spontaneous march, and everyone dropped what they were doing and followed the monks up to the temple to see what was happening. I jumped onto someone's pickup truck to videotape the cheerful crowd and heard a shout—E La was coming out of a noodle shop with her mouth full. She put her bowl of breakfast noodles down and jumped onto the pickup truck to ride up to the temple. "Very interesting, ga," she said.

* * *

EVENTUALLY, I STUMBLED onto a way to get the yearned-for song texts. Now living in a house with a kitchen and a dining table, I could finally repay some hospitality. Around a table laden with bowls of improvised dishes such as french fries and spaghetti marinara, I urged Aye Zai Guang, Aye Awn Noy, and other Tai Lües, "Eat more! What's the matter, don't you like foreign food?"

Suddenly, the men were deferring in an unfamiliar way. Tai Lüe women own their homes and men marry into them. By inviting the group over for dinner, I had placed myself in the position of a traditional hostess. I could compel the men to eat foods they found strange, urge them to drink a foreign alcohol to excess, and guilt-trip people who wanted to leave by acting personally wounded, just as they had with me.

Aye Awn Noy caved in first: "We warmly welcome you to study our Tai Lüe culture," he said. "Please tell us what it is you need, so that we can give it to you."

"I need more interviews with singers," I said. "And I would like to record a Buddhist oral poem in context, so that I can transcribe it and translate it into English."

"Why a Buddhist poem?" asked Aye Awn Noy.

"Because none of the books in Chinese about Tai Lüe oral poetry have any references to Buddhist poetry in them, and it seems from what Khanan Zhuai and others have said that in fact Buddhist oral poetry is at the core of Tai Lüe oral traditions," I answered.

There was a long pause. "Hm," said Aye Awn Noy to Aye Zai Guang, "that's a problem of atmosphere." They both looked away.

Clearly, the men were concerned about any one of a number of things: the risk of cultural appropriation or the danger of combining two incendiary elements—foreigners and an ethnic Buddhism. They had not survived this long by being naive.

However, there was perhaps some benefit to them in getting their beloved Buddhist oral poetry on record outside the country and increasing its visibility. China was definitely opening, after all—the question was, how far? Would it tolerate a foreign book that brought the semi-underground Buddhist revival and cultural expression into public view?

A few nights later, Aye Awn Noy climbed into the van after a long night of eating and drinking and snapped, out of the blue, "First the Hans came to oppress us and now the foreigners have come to oppress us." Then he leaned against the window and went to sleep.

A few days after that, Aye Zai Guang was on the phone. "Come on over, ga! We're all going to Da Menglong to see the promotion of six monks to the status of *khuba*. We'll be there for a few days. We're just waiting for you." He added, "There will be singers, and I've arranged for you to record them."

* * *

KHUBA (IN THAI, "*khruba*") are the senior masters in Tai Lüe monastic life. Some of Sipsongpanna's past khuba wrote classic texts on literature, history, and religion. Most monks who reach the age of forty in the Tai Lüe world are now automatically promoted to the status.

But Sipsongpanna's monks were mostly under the age of thirty—despite his authoritative air, my own teacher was only twenty-two. In 1998, there were a few *khuba* near Meng Hai, on the western border, but none had been promoted within Sipsongpanna. This ceremony marked the coming-of-age of revived Tai Lüe Buddhism.

About 5,000 people came to see the three-day *khuba* ritual. On the first day the six monks involved shaved their heads, put on clean orange robes, and went into meditation. On the second day they gathered in the town of Da Menglong for a ritual bathing and blessing by male elders who were former monks. They climbed on brightly-painted wooden *asana* (beds like divans), and the villagers carried them on their shoulders to an old temple downtown. They spent that night fasting and meditating while villagers arrived in throngs and laid stacks of food, money, and presents in front of them. The promotion ceremony took place on the third day.

From the outside, Da Menglong looks like any rural Chinese town, with shabby concrete buildings, dusty streets lined with tractor repair shops, and an air of quiet desperation. Historically, though, it is a key town on Sipsongpanna's borders, lying on the route to Kengtung and other Mekong capitals. That day there was a hectic feeling in the air. Men wore their finest fedoras, polyester pants, and sandals and milled around in small crowds, looking up and down the road. A few of the older men were standing in the middle of the street, banging tiredly on cymbals and gongs. Some palm fronds stuck up from the divider in the middle of the road.

The procession gathered before the temple gates. First, a cluster of village men carrying a monk seated on an *asana*. He wore orange robes, shoulders and head bowed, and he sat deep in meditation. A few tractors rolled by, and some loud, heavy, long-distance trucks that were carrying lumber out of Burma. The monk stayed in his concave pose, bowing in the dust floating up from the street.

A crowded alley led to the sheltered temple in back. At the mouth of the alley, hundreds of pairs of rubber sandals cascaded around the entryway. Hundreds of people stood backed up against the alley wall, squatting on their heels or standing and staring, holding children to their sides or on their shoulders, or poised with baskets of popped rice, ready to murmur "sa, sa" and throw the rice at monks as they passed. Further in, the front of the procession was waiting to fit into the temple, which was already crowded. Two young men stood in the courtyard with oversize conch shells, blowing them from time to time.

Inside, the temple was dark. Handmade trees with two-yuan notes for leaves, plates of food, and wicker tables spilling over with offerings blocked the view. What little light there was came from hundreds of handmade yellow candles, which dripped wax across the floor. Every inch of the floor was covered with women, children, legs, arms, and baskets of food. In the back, barely visible in the glimmering light, senior monks visiting the ceremony had spread out mats and lay curled up, napping. The six monks to be promoted would sit here in meditation all night.

As Donald Swearer comments of rituals in Thailand, rituals like this one "[establish] a common thread of meaning inherent in most Buddhist rituals, and in so doing [the ritual] connects the founder with past and present, the dead and the living."[1] To connect Tai Lüe monks and lay worshipers with past monks and worshipers, however, was an indirectly subversive act linking present worshipers with some in the past who had suffered persecution, as well as with those who had lived in an at least nominally independent kingdom. This previously banned ritual revived a dead lineage of Buddhist consecration and invoked a community that cut across time and geography.

* * *

WHILE MONKS AND laypeople gathered at the temple to prepare for the ritual, we were, inevitably, at another feast and about to be caught up in one of the indigenous lobbying efforts that were part of these celebrations.

Aye Zai Guang and Aye Awn Noy had hired their friend the driver and his van for the weekend, and along the way from Jinghong to Da Menglong we kept stopping to pick up people, mostly women in long dresses and sun-hats carrying big baskets of food. Eventually, all the seats in the van were taken by pilgrims and some younger guys had to sit on the floor, which they did with good humor. About a half-hour outside of Da Menglong the van began to slow as Aye Zai Guang peered out the window. He was looking for our lunch stop, an empty concrete building that looked to be a long way from nowhere. A man ran out onto the street and waved to us, and we descended from the van. As Aye Zai Guang and our host, the village chief, chatted enthusiastically in Tai Lüe, women in sarongs and with hair buns began to appear carrying folding tables, wooden stools, and then lunch: steaming bowls of beef, spinach, cabbage, chicken, nammi salsa, and plastic bags of sticky rice. From the village hidden up the hill emerged dozens of men, wearing their hats low over their eyes, and the seating arrangement was shuffled and reshuffled in order of hierarchy, each time with a raising of toasts in Tai Lüe to the occasion.

More people stopped by on their way to the ceremony in Da Menglong. "Look at these ladies!" Aye Zai Guang said, pointing out two elderly women wearing floppy sun-hats and broad grins, who were leaning on the windowsill. "They've walked all the way from Meng La," a town a seven-hour drive from Da Menglong, near Laos. The ladies declined food or a ride to the temple. "We like to walk," they said, and off they went, waving their walking sticks.

Aye Zai Guang said it was time for us to go, but the village had another plan: now that we had been treated to hospitality, it was time for a trip to their temple. A village elder at the table whisked out some temple offerings—cotton cloths and homemade yellow candles—and proposed a merit-making visit to the temple. This was an offer Tai Lües could not refuse and so the group left the dishes for the women to clean up and trooped up the hill. A young senior monk was summoned from his afternoon nap to receive our donation and we entered the main temple hall to pray, donate, and receive a blessing.

The entire male population of the village came in after us and sat down quietly, the women hovering at the doorway to listen. The monk took our offerings, chanted a rapid benediction, and a heavy silence fell.

The *bawchang*, the village layman in charge of the temple, cleared his throat and welcomed the "visitors from far away" to their village, one "so poor it does not even have a school." Then the village chief, our lunch host, elaborated. "Our town is indeed very poor," he repeated. "I hope someday our friends from far away, some even from other countries, will be able to help us. We need other people to speak for us because we cannot speak for ourselves. When we speak for ourselves, other people do not listen."

There was a rustling and a murmur of agreement from the crowd of women by the doorway.

"We have one hundred and ten houses and five hundred residents," the village chief continued. "For all those households, and all those children, we only have one school and one teacher. Now even that school is closed because our teacher got a job in Jinghong. The government has not sent a new teacher to replace her."

It appeared that Aye Zai Guang, whose wife was a high-ranking government official, was being put on the spot. He listened and answered that the government was very busy right now preparing for its annual elections. "When the new governor takes over in March he will probably have a new plan." He advised patience.

The village chief struggled to control his voice. "We have been to see the government eight times," he answered. "They are *always* too busy to meet with us. We take time from our work in the fields and travel to Jinghong to sit in their offices and wait for hours, but no one has time to talk to us. Meanwhile, our children are getting no education. How will this affect our future?"

Aye Zai Guang bowed his head and promised to do what he could.

As we walked down to the road, a girl of about ten with a quick grin and long braids followed alongside us, pushing and giggling with her friends. She mustered up enough courage to try a few words of Chinese on me. She spoke a little more Chinese than her mother did, and she was lively and bright. When we got back to the building where we had had lunch she showed me her Chinese notebook. Since the teacher left the girl had been studying on her own, trying to continue learning. "It's difficult," she said. "There isn't anyone around to practice with me."

She dragged me back to her house for tea, where her surprised mother apologized with some nervousness for her simple home and invited us to sit on a straw mat. She summoned her son, a twelve-year-old novice monk, to come down from the temple where he spent his afternoons and say hello. The senior monk at that temple, said the mother, was illiterate even in Tai Lüe and could not teach much. However, there was hope: "The former governor, Zhao Cun Xin, submitted my son's name to Wat Pajay," she said. "He's going to start his studies there this summer." At least one of her children would receive an education. While she spoke her daughter sat on the floor and idly drew Chinese characters in the dust with her finger.

We drove to Da Menglong to see the procession of the monks to the temple and Aye Zai Guang and his friends made a brief visit to a new reliquary under construction on the border. Then we returned to the village where we had eaten lunch so that Aye Zai Guang could spend more time talking to the chief. Dinner began not long afterward and continued for hours. The host had invited a changkhap but even I could tell he had poor rhyming skills and a voice mostly suited to singing bawdy songs to a crowd of men. Midway through the meal I stood up, thanked the host, and left the high-status chair beside Aye Zai Guang, over his objections. For the first time, I joined the women and girls sitting outside under the stars. Outside, there was no pressure to eat or drink, the atmosphere was relaxed, and the conversations revolved around clothes, the kids running around underfoot, and ribald jokes about the men inside.

Eventually, Aye Zai Guang rallied the driver and we went to the downtown temple where the narration by two changkhap of the Buddhist poem "Sithat auk boht" had been underway for almost an hour. He listened for a moment, then returned to the feast.

* * *

THE TEMPLE COURTYARD was paved with cool stone, full of a darkness rustling with breath, robes, and whispers. The moonlight filtering through palm trees showed hundreds of villagers—sitting and lying on the ground, leaning on the crooks of tree trunks, wrapped up against the evening dew, listening raptly. On the temple porch a young woman, the storyteller, sat cross-legged on the floor beside a man blowing a bamboo reed. She bowed her head over an open fan. The accompanist shook the spit out of his reed and blew a rippling melody as the woman sang,

Prince, heaui Prince, heaui. . . .

The door to the temple was shut and the six monks being promoted to *khuba* were sitting inside in meditation. It could be that
bits of the story filtered in, through the heavy wooden doors and
past the piles of offerings, to the monks on the wooden beds as they
worked to stay awake through the night.

E Ma was a renowned changkhap in her early thirties, slender,
with a hard face and large brown eyes, wearing a long, flowered
dress. Her voice was clear and slightly husky but it carried well. She
covered her face with a fan, eyes half-closed, and bowed into it to
focus on the tale.

The story she told was the familiar legend of the Buddha's quest
for enlightenment, with a few Sipsongpanna twists. Sakyamuni
(known as "Sithat" in Sipsongpanna and "Sitata" in northern Thailand) was born the heir to a wealthy clan of princes. Before he was
born, a fortuneteller said that he would become either a great king
or a great spiritual leader. This upset his father, who wanted Sithat
to be a prince and not a monk. The king did everything he could to
provide physical comforts while shutting the boy off from religious
influences. He ordered the finest silks, exotic animals, wonderful
foods, and great artists and musicians to entertain his son. When
Sakyamuni was old enough a marriage was arranged to a princess,
and they produced a son. But in the evenings Sithat began to won-
der about the world outside.

With the help of his groom (in Tai Lüe, named Nai Salathi),
Sithat slipped out of the palace grounds three times to see the outside world. On their first secret trip, he saw a man suffering from
illness and learned from Nai Salathi that all people are vulnerable to
illness. A few weeks later he and Nai Salathi ventured out a second
time; Sithat saw an elderly man and learned that all people get old
as well. On their third trip, Sithat saw a funeral and learned the fact
of death.

Sithat's father knew that something was seriously wrong and summoned beautiful dancing girls to the palace to seduce his son, but
they had no effect on the prince. Late that night, Sithat went to his
groom and woke him up. On their fourth trip out of the palace, Sithat

saw a barefoot monk. Nai Salathi said that the monk was seeking the secret of life and death. Sithat decided to follow his example.

When Sithat told this plan to his father, the king was dismayed and summoned his subjects to stay in the palace grounds and keep watch over Sithat. Our tape began here. E Ma sang,

> The father called on the masses and the courtiers,
> summoning them to travel together to this place,
> to surround and guard the wide-open palace.
> This was no small place,
> but outside, all around, even to the foot of the palace steps
> they slept there, they sat on guard,
> the great officials and noblemen led them and told them to
>   wait there.
> Now,
> the subjects took up machetes, bows and arrows, and so on,
> they paced back and forth guarding, out of fears for the
>   young prince.
> The palace doors were closed, locked up,
> until late at night when roosters crow,
> and a *tevata* came down to help.

As we had done with the earlier song by Khanan Zhuai, the monk and I translated this word-by-word. He transcribed the text in Tai Lüe and explained the meaning of each Tai Lüe word in Chinese. I wrote the meanings down in English and then read back the approximate sense of a line of verse in Chinese. We did this work on the wicker chairs in the receiving area of his quarters, shared with other monks. Some strolled in to listen from time to time and joined in explaining one or another Tai Lüe term or wandered out to do something else. Mostly, the room was quiet, and we were interrupted only by birds.

A *tevata*, said my teacher, is a Mekong Delta spirit with magical powers known for its generosity and goodwill; he pointed to a gold-plated statue of a *tevata* in the courtyard outside his rooms.

> [The *tevata*] whispered a spell to catalyze events,
> [it] entered quietly, with good words.

There was no way to get out, so the *tevata* came, cast a spell
that entered the [villagers'] heads and hearts,
making them all sleepy, drowsy.
The masses on guard, numbering not a few, collapsed in all directions where they stood,
even sleeping in pairs, leaning on one another,
like burned tree stumps in an Akha mountain field.

Akhas are one of the mountain peoples of the Mekong Delta. The
Akhas are notable, to the rice-farming Tai Lües, for practicing swid-
den agriculture. They burn sections of forest, leaving fields covered
with tree stumps, and then plant in the ground that has been made
fertile with ashes.

As daylight comes, it is dawn on the bare ground of the wide-
open palace,
deep asleep, a million women and men,
the tattoos on their bodies so thickly drawn that they do not feel
mosquito bites,
nor look for blankets on the grassy ground, but sleep soundly,
each one slumbers.
Now,
On the ground, all were sleeping, their bodies gray in the dawn
light like water buffalo.

"The tattoos keep them from feeling mosquito bites?" I asked.
The monks explained: Tai Lüe boys are tattooed at the age of
seven or eight with letters, sometimes with images of flowers or
birds. Usually the adults get a group of the kids drunk, and the
tattooing of ritual letters is a collective rite of passage. The tattoos cover one arm, sometimes extending to the chest and back.
These tattoos turn blue against the skin, and some of the letters
begin to fade with time. A man with many tattoos is believed
to be safer than one without them, and those who are covered
with tattoos say they are immune to mosquito bites—useful in a
region famous in Chinese historical annals for having both "tattooed wild men" and malarial swamps. These days the monks

discourage tattooing because of the risk of contracting the AIDS virus from unclean needles.

Back to the story: E Ma described Nai Salathi as preparing the prince's horse by saddling it up and muzzling it. The prince looked for the last time at his wife and child, asleep under the *tevata*'s spell, and said, "I must go," turning to his horse. As the horse approached the locked palace gates it leapt into the air and flew across, carried by invisible *tevata*. Nai Salathi grabbed the horse's tail and was carried along behind.

> As for the sleepers, once it was light,
> they sought for the Prince, but did not find Him.
> The palace was shut up tight as a fist,
> but nevertheless He got out.
> The people picked up a mallet and pounded the great
>   drum explosively,
> the people of the city-state all wept,
> they could not rest, they could not sleep.
> His wife and son were deeply hurt, grieving,
> they lay in bed and could not get up.
> Oh, now,
> They covered the head of the infant and lamented loudly,
>   weeping,
> "This pair of big eyes will not have a father to raise him."
> It was a very hard road to walk, for both grandparents
>   and child.
> Day and night they wept, day after day, without stopping.

Meanwhile, Sithat was greeted triumphantly by all the various gods of the Tai Lüe pantheon. The Sipsongpanna version skipped over the usual obstacles of Sithat's quest and took him directly to a sacred forest where he was met by a procession of gods. They spiraled down to earth in a solemn procession, carrying sacred objects such as long streamers and magical parasols, and as the men had done for the *khuba* arriving in this temple courtyard earlier in the day, the gods blew on conch shells to announce Sithat's arrival.

Sithat said, "Nai Salathi, follow Lord Wise Horse.

If you both return safely to my palace, then report to them that
all is well.

Go and tell [my father], and the precious pearl lady my wife,

that I have renounced my home and am deep in meditation."

Nai Salathi returned with Lord Wise Horse.

He gathered up all the horse's gear,

and he trailed the horse back toward the city-state.

Man and horse trudged the road together, reluctantly,

and when they stopped to rest, they wept together.

Now,

because that horse was rare, a jewel, a flower,

its eyes rolled back and forth in its head, and clear water fell
from its eyes,

and it died at the riverbank.

Lord Wise Horse's heart broke, and he died.

He died, leaving Nai Salathi a man alone in the world, without
friends.

Nai Salathi gathered up the horse's saddle in his arms

and turned his face back toward the city.

Dubi Gang, leaning against the doorway and listening with novices as we worked through the story, was moved. "Lord Wise Horse's heart broke, and he died," the senior monk said, and sighed. "E Ma of Muang Long is a good changkhap."

Sithat removed his princely robes and put on old, torn robes. According to tradition, a monk's robes were supposed to be made of rags taken from cremation grounds, "but mine come from Thailand," joked my teacher. Sithat sat under a tree and cut his long hair. This was swept up by the gods before it touched the ground and preserved in a dazzling pearl-studded stupa in the heavens, the Dom Gaun stupa whose name we had learned from Khanan Zhuai. Sithat sat under a tree on a pile of grass, which a deity magically transformed into a gold- and pearl-studded throne. He began to meditate.

E Ma concluded her chapter of the tale with some improvised lyrics praising her male singing partner, Aye Kham Naun:

Little sister is finished, so over to you, pearl brother,
I wait to hear your good narration. . . .
Little sister will sit and wait with these noble men.
I may forget myself in such honored company.
One more moment, I implore you [all] to wait for the noble
   Kham Naun,
Please continue to help me; you agreed to help speak for me.
I have made so many mistakes because there are so many
   people here . . .
How dare I speak before these guests?
How dare I sit before this patron, this former monk,
with a kind heart, this former abbot,
a man of high rank, who once ruled over a temple.
This great patron can discourse on any subject,
combining multiple genres in one poem . . .
and that's the way it is.

She sat back and cooled off. The large audience had made her nervous, perhaps especially the presence of a foreigner with a tape recorder. She had repeated a verse of her song by mistake and fumbled to find her place before Aye Kham Naun prompted her to continue. Overall, though, her throaty voice was moving, her lyrics were fluent, and her clear and poetic descriptions evoked another time and place.

During this break, some of the elders sitting beside her nudged one another and murmured an exchange. They pulled out a short, curved marimba about a foot-and-a-half long, mounted on a frame painted to resemble the body of a bird, and played an old, ritual melody, humming along with it quietly. Shot glasses were filled, cigarettes lit. The senior guests sitting on the temple porch around the singers passed around fruit bowls filled with mangoes, papayas, and sweet sticky rice wrapped in leaves. One or two people got up from the inner circle and left, and another few squeezed in, greeting the group and giving me a surprised stare. They pushed the microphone over to Aye Kham Naun.

Aye Kham Naun had a well-lined face and wore a plain plaid shirt and dark polyester pants. He appeared authoritative and was about fifteen years older than E Ma. As was the custom with professional singers, he had brought his own accompanist to blow the reed. E Guang had once mentioned that in the course of an evening's eight-hour performance she might change accompanists several times when they got tired, though she herself did not leave.

Aye Kham Naun cleared his throat and raised a fan in front of his face. His accompanist shook saliva out of his flute, mopped his forehead, and began to play.

Prince, heaui prince, heaui . . .
Now, listen, lady, who is able to blow such a great tornado:
Oh, how old I am,
too old to sing with you all, who are gathered here.
Now, I feel terrible,
I am just an old man who uses meat to soak up his liquor,
only good for teasing and tickling my sons and grandchildren
and making them giggle.
Now,
just suppose big brother were to come courting this woman,
who already has two or three lovers,
suppose I go and try to sweet-talk her?
I want to practice courtship,
I've been studying the way others go about it.
I would like to sell off a big pig and use all the money to buy
   you clothes and jewelry, and a little parasol that folds up.

At Wat Pajay, our translation was going slowly because some of the lines were not very grammatical. "This singer isn't as good as E Ma," said my teacher. "The bit about the parasol, that's a silly line." He played it again and frowned over it, listening. The deputy abbot, who had arranged these lessons, stuck his head in the doorway to see how we were doing, and frowned.

"What are you two doing in here? Singing love songs?" He tried to make this sound like a joke, but it was not.

My teacher flushed indignantly. "We are not singing love songs. We are translating 'Sithat auk boht [Sithat enters the monkhood]'."

"Senior monks are not to sing," said the deputy abbot.

"I'm not singing. I'm teaching her Tai Lüe. It's 'Sithat.'"

The deputy abbot shook his head and walked out.

I cleared my throat. "Should we stop?"

"Continue," said my teacher, hitching his robes around his shoulders and pushing his glasses up the bridge of his nose. He poured more hot water in our glasses.

   . . . and a little parasol that folds up.

Now,

How I long to take you as my girlfriend,

To show you off and make other women jealous.

This guy wishes he had a stomachache,

so I could ask you to rub my head.

I wish I could curl up and sleep by your side, with your arms
   around me.

Now,

Once upon a time, there was nowhere slack on my body that
   you could pinch.

Now—

A group of tourists from Sichuan in yellow baseball caps wandered by, admiring Wat Pajay's flowers and statues. A few peered into the monk's room where we were studying. One of the tourists, wearing a camera around his neck, walked right in as if the room were part of the tourist display, examining the robes hanging to dry over the dormitory beds, the stack of books on Buddhism, and the papers scattered over the table between us.

"Look," said the tourist to his friend. "The monk has a foreign girlfriend."

"Well, you know what they say—ethnic minorities are more 'open,'" the other replied. They strolled out. My teacher stared expressionlessly into space.

"Listen," I said, "why don't I ask someone else to help me translate this?"

"Like who?" he asked. I tried to think of non-monks in Jinghong able to read classical Tai Lüe and speak Mandarin.

"This is part of our Tai Lüe culture and you should know it," he said. "Stop procrastinating and read the next line." We bent over the text again.

Aye Kham Naun sang,

The people who crowd into this wide-open courtyard,
They have walked great distances, coming in wave after wave,
they swept up all the roads around to make them clean—

In the midst of his song, there was a noisy rustle at the back of the crowd in the courtyard. A few Tai Lües and a Han Chinese man of about thirty climbed into the circle, and everyone in it tensed. The Chinese man was cheerful with drink, having made the rounds of a series of village feasts like the one I had left. Surprised to see a foreigner in this gathering who could speak Chinese, he introduced himself: He was the Communist Party Secretary, the highest-ranking official in the Da Menglong area. The Party Secretary did not speak Tai Lüe; he was an educated young man about my age, and perhaps he had not been in the area very long. He beamed around at the crowd and then began to question me in a normal speaking voice while Aye Kham Naun continued to sing.

"What are you doing?" he asked, pointing at the cassette recorder.

"I'm taping the tale," I whispered. I didn't want to alienate the Party Secretary, but it had not been easy to get into this performance.

"What's the point of that?"

"I'm going to write it down and translate it into English."

This surprised him. "What for?"

"To put it in a library in America."

"Do you actually understand this stuff? I don't understand a word!"

Aye Kham Naun sang,

Now,
The Communist Party has come to lead the way again,
The Party Secretary has come to sit here,
he sits for a long spell, making up half of a happy pair—

a young lady chats with him politely.
Whoever enters this place today, may he live to a ripe old age!

"He is praising you," one of the elders across the circle said to the Party Secretary in Chinese.

"He's saying good things about you!" said another elder, loudly.

"Thank you!" said the secretary, folding his hands together in a *wai* to the singer. He sat fidgeting for another few minutes, then reeled out mid-lyric to go to another banquet. The gathering visibly relaxed, closing the circle again. No one had gotten into trouble, and the performance could go on.

* * *

AYE KHAM NAUN picked up the thread of the story where E Ma had left off. Because Sithat was sitting on this magical throne, meditating, a rival and malicious deity in the heavens (in Tai Lüe known as "Lord Man") began to fear that Sithat would "become king of the world" and rule from his magical throne. So Lord Man tried to get Sithat off the throne. First he tried by sending his beautiful, sultry daughters to seduce the meditating prince. They flew in wearing jewelry—necklaces and bracelets—and taunted the monk:

So the first woman hustled around and tore off her skirt;
another woman bustled about and stripped off her clothes,
took them all off;
another woman bared her belly and her lovely white breasts;
and another showed her white leg,
fat and wrinkled like an elephant's trunk;
they rolled around on the ground, hoping to seduce and
  touch Him;
they wanted to embrace Him and make Him their husband.
They sang a pretty song, sweet as sticky rice,
to melt the heart of the Buddha.
Sithat ignored them; He told those girls,
"You are evildoers, you are idiots."

Now,

"Those bodies of yours are only skin and meat, bones and muscle;
they smell, they reek of shit and piss."
At this, the sisters paled, turned yellow, bruised,
their hair, slicked back and styled in waves, turned straight,
white and cracked;
their teeth fell out, they became bags of skin and bones,
thin, haggard, hunchbacked, and weary;
they limped away with canes . . .
and could not find their way back up to the heavens.

Lord Man, having failed in his first assault, summoned warrior
demons from the heavens:

The troops were ordered to gather and prepare for battle.
He told them to put on armor and descend swift as a waterfall,
with cannons, bows and arrows, spears. . . .
The warrior troops busily prepared to fight,
they raised dust that made the heavens black like storm clouds.
Lord Man took the lead, seated on a mighty elephant:
Akhala! So fierce, wicked as a devil!
So fierce that one breath sets the trees on fire!
He muttered a murderous incantation,
lifted a giant boulder and hurled it into the sky,
where it split into pieces, falling on the head of the Buddha.
Now,
when the shards fell near the Prince,
they were transformed into silver raindrops,
a golden rain scattered around Him, and Sithat ignored it all.
When Lord Man saw this,
he was enraged, maddened, and he gibbered like an idiot.

Finally, sang Aye Kham Naun, Lord Man tried his last resort. He
demanded that Sithat provide proof that he had the rights to the throne
on which he sat. Sithat thought "busily," says Aye Kham Nawn, and
then, recollecting all his past lives in a flash, he answered,

"It is said that there are witnesses in the water—
Please, good people, come to my aid."
Nang Tholani emerged, and came to the side of the precious
  throne,
gazing up at His leg, His alms bowl, and the throne.

Nang Tholani is represented in many Tai Lüe temples as a small statue of a woman in a form-fitting dress. Her statue is usually only a few feet high. Kneeling at the Buddha's left hand in the temple, she is shown pulling out her long, fluid black hair from its bun in the act of saving the Buddha. Statues of Nang Tholani also appear in Laos and Thailand.

She bowed to Him on the throne and sat . . . unrolling her hair.
It became water, pouring out,
a vast waterfall with tidal waves flowing and crashing,
even knocking over trees, turning them into stacks of floating logs,
all of Lord Man's followers were swept away, and it was over.
Now,
at that moment, the precious one triumphed over the three worlds,
and thus was able to pass on the great stories of His past lives.
Now,
the precious one was able to triumph over His physical body,
arriving at enlightenment, becoming the Buddha.

In his enlightenment, Sithat discovers four truths that become the core of Buddhism. First, he concludes that all life is transient and therefore unsatisfying. Second, he says that the dissatisfactions are caused by human attachments to people and things that they are bound to lose. Third, the only way to escape this quandary is to cut it off at the root, to end attachments. Fourth, he concludes that forms of moderate self-discipline, such as meditation, can train practitioners to end attachments and pave the road to nirvana, the extinction of the self and the end of the cycle.

Having attained enlightenment the Buddha traveled widely, Aye Kham Naun concluded, arriving eventually at his home kingdom where he was greeted by the king and his family. His wife offered

him their infant son, head shaved, wrapped in orange robes, to be
a novice monk as well. "I will go to be a monk with the prince, my
father," said the infant.

Aye Kham Naun finished with a few lines of praise for E Ma:

Now, big brother came prepared to know and discourse on Sithat,
and this concludes this section of the tale.
Now it is my turn to rest,
You love me, hey . . .
In a moment, you radiant little sister, you flower,
you will tell me that you love me, but must keep your distance,
and so it goes.

The story was over but the crowd would not allow the two singers to leave, and with the encouragement of the crowd, the poetry
and the romantic dueling continued for hours. They sang until they
were hoarse, until E Ma coughed between every line. One of the accompanists began to waver, and another took over for him. Still, the
crowd, mostly women, urged them on to new poetic heights.

Older Tai Lüe women tend to be the biggest fans of changkhap,
and the women in the audience sat silent and radiant throughout.
They sat through the contradictory lyrics about women tempting
monks with their bodies and saving them with their sensuous hair,
through the demure flattery and the raunchy praise. Through all
the contradictory messages about women and Buddhism, they sat
with beaming smiles at the rare treat of hearing a couple of good
storytellers in their own language.

When the two singers stopped, pleading exhaustion, it was 2
a.m., and the crowd in the courtyard had thinned to maybe fifty
listeners who implored the tired changkhap for just one more
poem—one more.

Aye Zai Guang had slipped back onto the porch to catch the end
of the performance. We approached E Ma to congratulate her and
Aye Kham Naun on the six-hour performance. I asked how to write
her name in Tai Lüe. "I don't know," she answered apologetically.
"I am not literate." She and the other performers hurried away to
have dinner.

* * *

THE RITUAL PROMOTION of the six monks took place on the following day in a three-hour ceremony. At dawn, the sounds of firecrackers, cheers, and gongs in the Da Menglong street announced the start of the ceremony at the temple, where soon the monks were carried out into the crowded courtyard in a hail of popped rice. They were helped, weak with hunger and legs numb from sitting, up the stairs to a handmade platform. Then they were handed through a shelter covered in orange cloth, where the actual promotion rites were screened from the crowd. When they emerged, each wore a crown and glittering robes, and they were carried into the temple to eat their offerings. By midday the six monks were enthroned on the backs of jeeps, trucks, or tractors, surrounded by cheering villagers, shielded from the dust of the roads with palm fronds and carried home to their villages for more feasting and celebration.

Sipsongpanna now had its own senior Buddhist teachers again for the first time in fifty years. Tai Lües had mobilized themselves to revive long-hidden cultural traditions and build a locally controlled educational system that had finally produced new, local masters. The movement also had the power to sway Tai Lüe officials from Jinghong to help get a village a new teacher and, perhaps also the skill to manage the Party itself with well-timed praise.

* * *

OVER THE NEXT several months, with the help of Aye Zai Guang and others, I was able to meet and interview more singers and record other songs. With Aye Zai Guang's encouragement, one master singer, Aye Saut, showed off an impressive private library of song texts written on parchment, and another showed a notebook of crib notes for song performances—a Tai Lüe promptbook. We sought out and recorded singers in their nineties who remembered performing at temple openings in Thailand and apprentice singers as young as twelve who sang passionate love songs (fig. 18). We were even reluctantly given song texts to copy, narrative poems that instructed listeners in the old Tai Lüe political system and that laid out moral

18 *A teenage* changkhap *accompanied by her teacher, Aye Saut, on the reed. The* posters on the wall of her home show Chinese pop stars.

precepts. We heard other narrative poems, composed for Songkran, that foretold the weather and harvests for the coming year.[2]

The recording of Sithat's quest for enlightenment, the narration of "Sithat auk boht" looms above all these as one evening that brought together past and present. Sithat's tale of leaving behind material comforts in search of freedom echoed the gradual emergence of an ethnic religious movement from behind the scenes and into the light, even as the telling helped this to happen.

***

SONGKRAN HAD COME and gone, along with the crowds of visitors and wild parties, tourist and local, that accompanied it for a month before and after. Villagers had celebrated the holiday for weeks with feasting and competitions for firing off handmade rockets. In Jinghong the holiday was celebrated with a massive overhaul of the city, with city employees draining and clearing out the lake in the middle of downtown, sweeping the streets, and jailing suspected drug users and street people to make sure there were no disruptions during the big festival. Thousands of visitors came to town, including high-ranking officials from Beijing and journalists from Europe and Japan, to watch villagers compete by racing their rowing boats decorated with painted dragon heads across the Mekong. Wat Pajay celebrated with the ritual cleansing of the Buddha image, attended by the governor of the prefecture, who took the opportunity to dump an auspicious bottle of water down the back of my neck.

And then it was the day of Songkran itself. The whole city locked down as the streets were taken over by roving bands of drunken men, who ganged up to gleefully dump drowning bucketfuls of water on any passing victims, especially women or foreigners. At the end of the day, one of the employees at Chunhuan Park unchained the depressed elephant that posed for photos with tourists all year and rode the elephant galloping and trumpeting down Jinghong streets.

As the holiday receded into the past and Sipsongpanna residents recuperated in quiet, the weather became increasingly muggy. I biked out to the temple one humid day in early June for Tai Lüe language class, and my monk teacher and I bent over the last few pages of "Sithat auk boht."

"There," said the monk, as we concluded the translation. "Are you satisfied? Now you have a real Buddhist oral poem."

As he spoke, he stood up to look out the window. Over the valley was a wall of black clouds streaking to the ground—the first rain of the monsoon season. Within a few minutes it was on us, like a bucket of water being dropped from the skies. It battered the roof and smashed at the wooden shutters as we hurried to close them. With the shutters closed, the room became dark and full of the sounds of outside splattering.

"So what about you?" I asked. "How did you decide to leave home and become a monk?"

"I was ten years old," he answered. His parents had divorced when he was a toddler and he had lived with his mother for a while in her village. A few years later, his father, who had remarried, decided that this was not a good arrangement and took custody of him. Not long after, my teacher decided that he would become a monk. His family had often noticed signs of his piety from infancy, he said, but the real reason he decided to initiate was that the other kids were doing it and "I thought being in the temple would be fun." He went to live with his uncle and aunt, who sponsored his initiation and gave him preliminary training for the temple. At first he served at the temple in the village where his uncle and aunt lived. Eventually he was sent up to Wat Pajay, which had been reopened in 1990.

"When I started, it was just because I thought it would be fun. But as I got deeper into it, I began to get more out of Buddhism, so then I took the vows and became a full monk."

"But as a child, you couldn't have known what you were choosing to do," I said. "It's not like ordaining as an adult. How can anyone ask a child to make such a big choice?"

"Your reasons for doing something change as you get deeper into it," he said. "Maybe the things that led you to start studying Chinese in college are different from the things that interest you in China now. Why wouldn't it be the same for us?"

Anyway, this was a monk with worldly ambitions, not a natural ascetic. The temple had given this farmer's son a free education. It had taught him to use computers, even Macintoshes, and had won him a scholarship place in college in Kunming. There he had earned his associate's degree in business administration; he was the first in his family, his village, and his temple to get a college degree of any kind. His gratitude to the temple was genuine. He often liked to boast that of the five monks that Wat Pajay had sent up to Kunming, only he had not succumbed to the big city's temptations and defrocked. This monk resisted temptation and came back to Jinghong still wearing the saffron robes. He was the only college-educated, Chinese-speaking monk at the central temple in Sipsongpanna—in a way, he was their hot shot.

These were opportunities not available to the Tai Lüe women I knew at Journey to the East: because the temple would not initiate girls as novices, they could not have the education in classical texts or the opportunities to study in Thailand. One Tai Lüe woman began to study old Tai Lüe script at the temple privately, after I had done so, but she had to leave in order to keep working her full-time job. Still, just as those women lived with the pressure to be the lithe, beautiful Tai Lüe maidens promised in the tourist brochures, the young men at the temple faced their own contradictory pressures.

Sometimes his community's expectations and his own high expectations for himself seemed to weigh heavily on my teacher. He spoke constantly of defrocking and returning to secular life, but who would employ a former senior monk with no other work experience? When our language classes started, there had been talk of a prestigious post in a local policy bureau, but since then Beijing had imposed a nationwide hiring freeze on civil servants, so that was out. He wanted to stay in Jinghong, but after all that religious and secular education how could he just work as a manager at a hotel, open a restaurant, or join the army—the only career options for an educated person? Even his cutting-edge Macintosh skills were only useful in the temple.

The dark side of the Buddhist revival was that while their temple education gave monks like my teacher an elite status among Tai Lüe villagers, it did little to prepare monks for the world beyond the temple that they would eventually join. The day a senior monk defrocked at the age of twenty-five or thirty, the high status he had known since childhood evaporated, leaving him a child in an adult's body. Suddenly, he was a thirty-year-old man with no experience of jobs, financial responsibility, or women, and no identity or status aside from the one he had left behind. The gifted monk I had chatted with in Thai and English on that first day at the temple was a tragic example. Fluent in several languages and talented in computer design, he had left monastic life and married a local woman that year. Unable to find a job in Jinghong, he began doing freelance cross-border trade with people his wife knew in Burma and Laos. He smuggled drugs once, got caught, and wound up doing two years of hard labor in a Kunming prison camp.

And, ironically, the Chinese college education that was the most marketable part of my teacher's training had set him apart from the other monks at Wat Pajay. Some of them spoke of him behind his back, saying that his years in Kunming had made him too proud. They said he was more comfortable speaking Chinese than the language of his own people.

"You are alone in Jinghong," he said, "and I am alone at Wat Pajay."

Conclusion
Buddhas on the Borders

A coda to the *khuba* ceremony in Da Menglong:
      At one point during that festival weekend our van was en route to the temple in Da Menglong to watch another stage in the ceremonies when Aye Zai Guang leaned over the back of his seat and said, casually, "By the way, we're going to Burma. A famous monk, Khruba Bunchum, is building a reliquary for us Sipsongpanna Tai Lües across the border, and we're going to pay our respects to him."

Tai Lües in Sipsongpanna are continually going over the border into Shan State—for business, for family celebrations, or just because they feel like it and someone they know has a car with room for one more. "That sounds nice," I said. "When will you go?"

"Now," he smiled. "We're all going to Burma, right now."

The Burmese border was a few miles from Da Menglong, but this trip had not been on the agenda. "It's not legal for Americans to cross the border from China into Burma. I didn't even bring my passport!"

"No problem," he waved his hand. "Relax, ga. We're just going for half an hour. We do this all the time."

Unsurprisingly, the Chinese border guard did not see it that way. Spotting a large blond head in the van full of smaller, dark ones, he ran out of his office, waved his gun at the driver, and insisted everyone disembark. But he soon accepted my name card and Aye Zai Guang's copious apologies, then waved the van full of Tai Lües across the border crossing for an hour's visit to the new reliquary.

I was officially confined to the sweltering porch of the border station for the duration. Foreigners aren't allowed inside border station buildings because, presumably, they could steal valuable secrets, such as the fact (learned by listening at the door) that the guards are playing cards. While the soldiers gambled away the afternoon, I sat on the porch and watched rivers of Tai Lüe and Akha pilgrims, farm laborers, and traders pour back and forth in and out of Burma with no more procedure than a cheery wave in the direction of the building. In an hour, Aye Zai Guang's van came back, and everyone in it was radiant about meeting with Khruba Bunchum, the Burmese Tai Lüe monk.

This sight of floods of Tai Lüe Buddhist pilgrims crossing the borders in both directions stayed with me, and a few years later I noticed a news report that struck the chord again. In February 2002, BBC News reported that the Chinese government was completing construction on a statue in Tibet. The statue was to commemorate Tibet's liberation by the People's Republic of China—echoes of that monument to Sipsongpanna's liberation in the Jinghong theme park. But the Tibetan statue was being built directly in front of the Potala Palace, the former home of the Dalai Lama and a site sacred to Tibetans. Exiled Tibetan activists decried the statue, of course, calling it "a reminder of their humiliation." In Tibet, Yunnan, and (I would soon learn) Burma, authoritarian states were building highly contested monuments in Buddhist borderlands, while ethnic peoples were reviving transborder Buddhism that subverted the claims of states. Why all this Buddhist activity on the borders?

The construction of China's "front stage" ethnic displays and Buddhist tourist destinations had justified China's political expansion from center to borders and had literally paved the roads to the appropriation of massive material resources in both Yunnan and Burma. The lack of political rights or equal economic opportunities in any of this rapid development for ethnic minorities had driven some to revive and reinvent a transborder network of their own. That meant creating an "imagined community," an ethnic identity to justify the network.

Now the Tai Lüe Buddhist revival in Sipsongpanna clearly reached beyond China's borders, linking the Tai Lües in Jinghong with cous-

ins and colleagues in Laos, Thailand, and Burma. Monks were crossing back and forth more often, and there seemed to be a growing
number of Buddhist temples and reliquaries on all sides of the shared
national borders. Increasingly, I was hearing monks in Jinghong talk
about Khruba Bunchum, the Burmese Tai Lüe monk who lived near
Kengtung and traveled Southeast Asia by foot. Many Tai Lües in Jinghong wore his amulets. He was part of a growing network of linked
peripheries around the Mekong Delta—a network of Buddhas. Was
this a pan-Tai nationalist revival, and if so where would it lead?

* * *

EXPLORING THIS TRANSBORDER network posed a serious logistical problem: How to have a close look at the pan-Tai activity without getting
myself or local Tais in trouble? The border was porous and physi-
cally easy to cross—in some areas of Sipsongpanna it was so poorly
marked that foreign backpackers often crossed over unknowingly.
But if I didn't get detained on the Chinese side of the border, where
I might be interrogated and banned from the country for good, I
could get jailed on the Burmese side. Burma was a pariah country
ruled by a military junta, where corrupt soldiers were capable of
throwing a foreigner in a jail cell to rot if she didn't have the means
to bribe her way out. Neither option was appealing.

However, the forces of globalization were pushing on the borders
as well. Within a few years, the Thai and Burmese governments
opened their shared border at the Thai town of Mae Sai and the
Burmese town of Tachilek, and the states began to allow foreign
tourists to cross. Foreign tourists could travel north in Shan State
for five days as far as Kengtung, the town Jinghong Tai Lüe monks
and pop singers had spoken of so often. The only problem was that
a foreigner had to leave her passport at the Burmese border station,
traveling only with a photocopy stamped by the border guards. If
something went wrong—if, for instance, you got close to a group of
suspected Tai separatists and a spy reported this to the military—
you were stuck in a no-man's-land with nothing but a photocopy
to wave at the soldiers. That would be bad, but the fate of the Tais
would be worse.

Taking a very short trip, though, and some precautions, the worst-case scenario could probably be avoided. After a few more visits to Jinghong and a short trip to Laos, I obtained another research grant. I spent a few months in Thailand in the summer of 2000 working with exiled Burmese ethnic activists on their research into environmental problems in Burma and learning from them about Shan State. Then I took the bus up to Mae Sai for a short trip to Kengtung. By the end of the trip I began to see all the buddhas—those built by governments and those built by Tai activists—as sitting in the middle of larger struggles over material resources and political power.

China and Burma

MUCH HAD CHANGED in recent years along the Chinese-Burmese border—a region that some called the "golden triangle," and the source of much of the world's heroin. Having more or less completely deforested Yunnan and mined its gold and minerals, China was now reaching into Burma for much-needed material resources. China also needed access to the global shipping routes that Burma could provide. To gain access to opportunities in Burma, Beijing first had to help Burma conquer ethnic rebels. China's carrot-and-stick approach to ethnic groups in Yunnan had successfully brought that region under control; now it began to ship arms and funds to Burma to pacify the same peoples across the national borders.

For decades, much of Burma had been occupied by ethnic armies fighting the Burmese military for independence. Shan State, the majority-Tai area in the northeast, had been home to several of these armies. It had also been a base for some time of the Kuomintang insurgency against China, supported at least in part by the U.S. CIA. In turn, the Chinese government under Mao Zedong had trained and funded Maoist insurgencies based in Shan State that targeted Burma, bringing them occasionally into Yunnan for training and funding.

A democratic election in 1990 awarded the presidency to opposition leader Daw Aung San Suu Kyi. However, the military junta refused to hand over power to the opposition party. Instead, the ruling party changed its name from the State Law and Order Restoration Council to the State Peace and Development Council, changed the country's name from Burma to Myanmar, and declared a new beginning.

After the end of China's Cultural Revolution, Chinese support for the Burmese Maoists dwindled. Gradually, the two countries changed tack and became allies. As the world community turned its back on Burma, refusing to invest in Burma's economy because of its record of human rights abuses, China stepped in as the new patron that never questioned Burma's "internal affairs." Slowly, in the early 1990s, China began to arm Burma's military and to assist with training. At a critical moment when Burmese ethnic rebels appeared about to turn the corner, Chinese arms sales enabled an especially devastating assault on the Kachin army.[1] This led to a Kachin cease-fire with Burma, and other ethnic cease-fires followed.

Reports of human rights abuses—forced relocations of hundreds of thousands, if not millions, of ethnic peoples; extrajudicial killings of those suspected of aiding rebels; and the systematic use of rape as a weapon of war—did not diminish.[2] While most of the former rebel minority groups have signed cease-fires with the Burmese state, a breakaway faction of the larger Shan army has refused to cede.

In the wake of the cease-fires, and still working closely with China, Burma has launched a number of putative development projects in the borderlands, especially including tourism. Officials and entrepreneurs from Yunnan soon became involved in tourist businesses on the Shan State–side of the border, building new hotels, karaoke lounges, and restaurants. Others became involved in infrastructure projects, building roads and bridges in northern Burma. Soon, Yunnan's local agricultural products had found a new, faster shipping route to Europe that cut across northern Burma. By the late 1990s, China had an observation post in the Coco Islands in the Bay of Bengal, near Burma's western shore and strategically close to China's old enemy, India.

Growing fears of Chinese influence in Burma may have prompted the Association of Southeast Asian Nations to invite Burma to join in the late 1990s in an attempt to draw Burma away from that influence. At the same time, and for perhaps similar reasons, the

Asian Development Bank and the UN began to bring Burma into planning meetings for regional development projects. The lynchpin of these was an ambitious Asia Highway, with which the ADB and the UN planned to connect Southeast Asian cities with China and, someday, Central Asia. The highway, the ADB argued, would remove obstacles to international trade and promote sustainable development, including tourism, to benefit local peoples who lived along the highway. As in China, Burmese state-sponsored tourism development had in many ways been used to bless a larger project of state domination and control of resource-rich, strategically important ethnic borderlands.

I learned about much of this from Burmese ethnic activists in northern Thailand concerned about the impact of rapid economic growth on Burmese and Thai forests and rivers—and concerned about the resource grab that was displacing impoverished ethnic peoples from land rich with teak and gold.[3] Companies selling over the border to Yunnan and inland China, where the demand for tropical hardwoods was vast and growing, had logged huge swaths of northeast Burma.[4] Some of the activists recently arrived from northern Burma reported seeing hundreds of Chinese barges mining long stretches of Burmese rivers in ethnic regions. "They bring in big groups of Chinese workers to do the mining and none of them have visas or permits," said one. Others who had lived in the affected regions had seen companies dumping poisonous mining tailings back into the rivers. I was never able to confirm this, but a Tai Lüe friend from Yunnan said that Yunnanese government officials had cut deals with the Burmese military to engineer and build sections of the Asia Highway that ran through minority regions of Burma. In return, the friend said, Yunnan officials were promised exclusive rights to half the profits from any mineral deposits they found along the way. The other half would go to the Burmese military. Tai Yai, Tai Khun, Kachin, and Karen activists in northern Thailand expressed serious concerns over the Burmese government's use of rhetoric about economic development to justify the forced displacement of ethnic peoples and the removal of trees and minerals from their land.[5]

The state's involvement in restricting ethnic culture and its religious constructions in the Burmese borderlands were at the center

of these struggles. Tai exiles in Burma spoke of the Burmese government's ambitious project to build dozens of Buddhist temples
and reliquaries in ethnic regions of Burma, often on sites sacred
to local people. "They are fake temples and fake Buddhas," one
said. This was a term I had heard in Sipsongpanna, when Tai Lüe
laypeople and monks referred to one or another temple, popular
among tourists, as "fake." In the midst of transborder road-build-
ing, global shipping, tourism, mining, and logging, Buddhism was
emerging again as a site of contest between an authoritarian state
and ethnic activists.

Kengtung and the Golden Buddha

THE BORDER CROSSING between Mae Sai, Thailand and Tachilek, Burma
was like the mirror in *Alice Through the Looking Glass* that separated
the waking world from a dream world. On one side, a thriving Thai
market town, with rows of stalls selling herbs, teas, dried mush-
rooms, T-shirts, and electronic gadgets; on the other side, depressed
silence. On one side, glittering red-and-gold shop signs in Thai and
streets jammed with new cars and prosperous Thai tourists; on the
other, gray Burmese storefronts, dusty streets, thin people, trucks
of heavily armed soldiers, and shop signs that apparently had not
been repainted since the 1950s. On one side of the bridge were professional and methodical Thai immigration officials. On the other
was a smiling, deferential Burmese official who needed two hours,
several impromptu fees, and multiple packages of U.S. cigarettes to
photocopy a passport, lock it in his desk drawer, change U.S. dollars
into Burmese kyat at the uxorious official exchange rate, and stamp
a tourist-visa application.

It was also, he explained, his job to arrange my transportation
on the bus to Kengtung, which took him an additional half-hour.
In the end, the ride worked out well—the bus, it turned out, was
actually a tiny battered car driven by Tai Khuns who were happy
to speak Tai with a foreigner. In between, they skillfully navigated
mountain roads that were two-thirds mud and, with equal skill,
managed the five or six military checkpoints on the five-hour drive
from Tachilek to Kengtung. The mountain views along this route

were breathtakingly beautiful, in part because despite being resource rich, Burma is deeply impoverished.

E La had always insisted that Kengtung was "not very interesting, not worth the trip," but she and other Jinghong Tai Lüe friends who had downplayed its charms had seen it with different eyes. Kengtung is a valley town, built on winding hill roads that circle a small lake. Unlike Jinghong, Kengtung has many old buildings, including some churches built by British and American missionaries in the nineteenth century, temples that may date back thousands of years, and a few of the old Tai Lüe royal homes, now locked up. There was no electricity except for that created by private generators for hotels and the homes of wealthy generals. Looming over the town was a brand-new gold-plated statue of the Buddha, one of the many recently built by the Burmese military; it was also one of the ones Burmese Tais in Thailand had disparaged as "fake."

A local man with a motorcycle who hung around the marketplace offering tours agreed to take me up to have a look.

The Golden Buddha statue in Kengtung had replaced an ancient wooden statue commemorating the Buddha's legendary visit to Kengtung in which he reportedly struck his walking stick into the ground and declared Kengtung a good place to live, creating a lake. The crude features of the new statue are typical of those built in recent years in both Burma and Thailand and give the face of this statue a strange expression—from some angles it seems to have a smirk of condescension. The statue projects authority because of its size, gold leaf, and the fact that it is lit up at night though the city has no electricity for public use. Its base has Burmese lettering with the names of the generals who donated the funds for its construction.

To avoid any risk of repercussions to them, I had not asked Tai Lüe friends in Sipsongpanna for contacts in Kengtung and just trusted to luck. I moved around Kengtung talking with Tai Khuns, as well as a few Tai Lües who had moved to Kengtung from Sipsongpanna decades ago, and heard many speak of the obstacles they faced to practicing their culture and teaching their language. One couple pressed on me photographs of family members dressed in Tai Khun costume to take to Jinghong, saying, "Tell the people there that despite everything, we have managed to keep Tai ways here."

Another man unlocked the tombs of the last several generations of Tai Khun princes and showed me around the teak home of the brother of the last prince of Kengtung, so that if the military dynamited those too, there would be someone outside of Shan State who could describe them.

A third person, who had joined the Kuomintang and fought the Chinese army with them in the 1950s, said that back then, semi-independent Shan State had seemed like a better place to live than Maoist China had. Recently, though, he had been able to slip across the border into Sipsongpanna and see his sister for the first time in nearly fifty years. "Jinghong has skyscrapers now," he mused in half-remembered Chinese. "You can do any kind of business you want there. I wish I had stayed."

During these discussions many Tais complained about the Golden Buddha. The monks who care for it are not "real monks," said one, but government spies. Another Tai said that instead of the compassionate face of the Buddha, the statue had a "bad" expression and that it generated "bad" energy that made Tai people ill. The bad energy, they explained, comes from corrupted or inappropriate relics placed inside the base of the statue. Burmese Tais I had met in Thailand had claimed that the military's temples and statues were built with *yadaya*, a traditional form of Burmese magic that, as Aung Zaw described it, "is used to ward off evil spirits and weaken one's enemies."[6] A number of Burmese generals are known to practice *yadaya*, numerology, and astrology. For these Tais, an active malevolence lay at the heart of statues like the Golden Buddha. It seemed to be holding a destructive energy in its core. "There is a famous Tai Buddhist saint who has advised us not to look directly at the statue or it will make us ill," added one Tai Khun woman in Kengtung. Asked his name, the Tai Khun woman said it was Khruba Bunchum—the same Buddhist monk Aye Zai Guang and his friends had crossed the border into Burma to visit that day over two years earlier.

The Burmese military is building dozens of similar new temples around the country as a form of tourism development, but also as a way to invoke religious power behind the state and to underscore the state's legitimacy to a predominantly Buddhist population. Much of the recent nationwide Burmese effort to renovate and reconstruct older Buddhist images, temples, and reliquaries has centered on the nation's capital, Yangon, but the military has built dozens of new structures in ethnic minority regions as well. In addition to the Golden Buddha statue in Kengtung, according to Kachin refugees in Thailand, these structures include a new reliquary at the confluence of the Mali Hka and Me Hka Rivers, a local sacred site in the non-Buddhist Kachin state.

This temple- and reliquary-building project has been one of many major tourism development projects conducted across the entire nation. Burmese-government tourism development has included the restoration of monuments and urban areas, the repainting of residential homes, the construction of highways, ethnic theme parks, and hotels, and a range of beautification projects, all initially undertaken in preparation for "Visit Myanmar Year 1996." But, again, a number of these projects are linked to rights abuses, especially in areas of Shan State like Kengtung; the military has reportedly forcibly relocated ethnic peoples from tourist destination sites and has used forced labor for many of its projects.[7] The State Peace and Development Council responded to international criticisms in its state-run newspaper by asserting that Burmese people engage in "voluntary" labor in a Buddhist tradition of meritorious public works. Nonetheless, the widespread and confirmed reports resulted in the International Labor Organization's unprecedented condemnation of Burma for its use of forced labor and a devastating foreign boycott of tourism in 1996. Daw Aung San Suu Kyi continues to request the boycott.[8]

The SPDC's renovation and building projects invoke Southeast Asian Theravada Buddhist traditions of kingship, in which a Buddhist king built reliquaries around his realm, marking a "sacred topography" that unified his kingdom and sacralized his rule.[9] "The Buddha sacralizes the land," writes Donald Swearer, describing this Buddhist tradition. "He becomes the ground of political order and power, through his physical presence, his actual visitations, or symbols of his physical presence, i.e., his relics and his images."[10] According to this tradition, pious Buddhist kings built monuments to mark out the limits of their sacred empire; today, a military dictatorship follows suit, invoking traditions of Buddhist kingship by marking a sacred border.

Tais in Kengtung did not accept these claims, though; rather, they saw the state's monument as a symbol of oppression that actively destroyed local monuments. One said that the Golden Buddha statue points with its right hand over the lake at the center of the town, a gesture that "tells us Tai people to stay down, obey." One claimed he had seen helicopters siting the hand to point directly at the former palace of the Tai Khun prince. Not long after, the palace was demolished to make way for a new tourist hotel, over the objections of local Tai Khun monks and scholars. To curtail the debate, the chief of the police had dynamited the palace in the middle of the night. I met this police chief, and he urged me and other Western critics to forget about the incident and focus on the good that the SPDC had done for Kengtung Tai Khuns: "Tourism is tourism," he said, "and politics are politics." Not everyone in Kengtung agreed—photographs of the destroyed palace were reproduced and sold on the back streets as mementos.

Though one might expect Tais in Shan State to have more urgent preoccupations—hunger, unemployment, state violence—they held on to their right to say which monuments were real and which were fake, their language and script, and their temples as if these were the last defense of their dignity, the last location of dwindling Tai political autonomy. Burmese Tai rock singers such as Sai Mao, whom I interviewed by telephone from his home in Tachilek, spoke of using song and language to awaken a sense of Tai pride and unity in what he called "the Tai nation." Local temples in Kengtung held community meetings, rock-music concerts, and Tai Khun–language classes. In fact, it was Tai Khuns in this region of Burma who had invented the Macintosh font for printing the Tai script. They had gotten the font to refugees and activists in northern Thailand, who in turn gave it to Tai Lües from Sipsongpanna to take back to Jinghong. For these activists, ethnic culture, and with it religion, were not luxuries but central sites of resistance.

Back to Jinghong

THE PLANE FROM Kunming flew over the familiar sea of green whorls of tea bushes and the mist rolling along the muddy brown Mekong

River. When the plane landed in Jinghong I disembarked at a brand-new international airport terminal, flashing with steel and glass. Instead of being dumped unceremoniously from a pickup truck, passenger bags appeared on a new, black belt, and the floor of the terminal was waxed to a shine. But the terminal was empty.

I caught a taxi in the parking lot and was swept off along a capacious new highway over a breathtaking vista of rice fields, stilt houses, and purple mountains. This was part of the planned Asia Highway, built with funds from the Asian Development Bank and opened in 1998 with local fanfare. But today, it was empty too. It had been only four years since I had first arrived with those massive suitcases but this was a different town, in many ways a grimmer one.

As Mat, stubbing his finger on the batik tablecloth at Journey to the East, had foretold back in 1997, the development of Sipsongpanna for tourism had happened too quickly; it had imploded. The town's skyline was an impressive one, full of glinting glass and metal hotel high-rises, and the streets were now paved and clean. But the domestic tourists weren't arriving in droves the way they had in 1997 and 1998. As part of the gradual but inexorable opening of China's borders with Southeast Asia, China had officially allowed tourists to obtain visas to Thailand, and tens of thousands were pouring down there, armed with the still-strong Chinese yuan. Other tourists went north to Lijiang, where old Nakhi ethnic buildings had been preserved as a UNESCO World Heritage Site. The charms of Jinghong's dancing maidens had faded somewhat against the competition.

I checked into the decaying state guesthouse, the Xishuangbanna Binguan, noting that, whatever else had changed in Jinghong, at least the stains left on the walls by the 1997 monsoon were still the same. The first stop was, of course, the Journey to the East café. Anulan had found a job with an international environmental group and now lived in Amsterdam. Her cousin had inherited the shop. She leaned on the doorway and sighed grimly. "Business is bad. Foreigners don't stay anymore," she said. "They come for two days and go straight over the borders to Laos. There's nothing for them to see now." Where there had been rice fields in the land between downtown Jinghong and Wat Pajay, now there were street upon street of gleaming, empty three- and four-star hotels. I stopped in one on the pretext of renting a room and strolled through miles of orange-carpeted hallways, past air-conditioned room after air-conditioned room, all empty. Many more hotel buildings had been abandoned unfinished, their concrete infrastructures rotting in the tropical humidity. At the edge of town a Thai theme park, so vast that it spoke of a great vision not tethered to reality, sat hugely empty. There were no visitors to fill its stadium theatre, to rent its luxury condominiums, or to eat in its palatial restaurant overlooking a man-made lake. I biked back to Journey to the East along a long stretch of the Asia Highway, which lay baking quietly in the afternoon sun.

One by one, old friends arrived—E La, recently returned to Jinghong after a short sojourn with her boyfriend in Singapore, and Johnny Ma, a Han Chinese translator, who showed photos of his newborn son. I asked them what had happened to the rest of the town. E La shrugged and said, "They developed Sipsongpanna so fast, they stopped it." Johnny joked wryly, "Why come here to see fake Thais when you can go to Thailand and see the real thing?"

What did the future hold for Jinghong? Johnny thought things might improve in a few years when the Asia Highway was finally finished and long-distance truckers began to ply the route between Kunming and Bangkok. "But then we'll be a truck stop, with prostitutes and so forth. Things may improve, but they will never go back to the way they were."

As I moved around the town, I learned that the economic changes in the region were causing profound dislocation of local Tai Lües. Because of their minimal education and poor Chinese-language skills, many ethnic minorities had been on the fringe of the tourist boom when it peaked. Lacking the capital to build a hotel or buy a restaurant, they took positions as janitors, maids, or guards or engaged in small-scale trade around the periphery of the economy. When tourism began to decline they were the first to lose their jobs. Many young Tai Lües now were taking advantage of the open borders to move south to Thailand and try their hands at business there. But Thailand's tourist economy was not much better off than Sipsongpanna's after the economic crash of 1997, and when Chinese Tais could not find work there they moved on to other towns in the Mekong Delta.

A growing number of Tai Lües now pieced together a living in multiple cities around the borderlands—work a few months in a guesthouse, smuggle some fruit up the Mekong, translate for a traveling group of Chinese businessmen, and, as one said, "make a living anyway, anyhow." Political forces had dislocated Tais in Burma; a roller-coaster economy was dislocating more in China. Young Tais and other locals had become economic nomads, circling from town to town around the Mekong Delta, looking for the next big break.

Meawhile, Jinghong's Buddhist temple was thriving. Each time I visited, Wat Pajay had expanded slightly, building new classrooms, residences, and prayer halls. The monks had also expanded their printing projects: in 2002 they negotiated government permission and published the first dictionary in Chinese and old Tai Lüe. Demand for their old Tai Lüe Macintosh font was growing also—Tais in other parts of China wanted to see it and use it. As it strengthened its position in Sipsongpanna, the temple had begun to spin off minor industries of its own, including architecture, publishing, and even a small trade in Buddhist robes and icons.

Gradually, the Jinghong temple was gaining in strength and expanding in influence. Tai Lüe monks and laypeople in Wat Pajay, though, were insistent that their ethnic and religious revival was not a nationalist one; instead, it was aimed at building ethnic strength within the context of a developing, modernizing Chinese state. The monks seemed still able to manage local government astutely: with official permission, Wat Pajay arranged an annual one-day visit by the Burmese Tai Lüe monk, Khruba Bunchum.

Here was his image again—Khruba Bunchum. I had noticed photographs of this monk in temples around Sipsongpanna and had heard of him now from several people, including Aye Zai Guang and Tais in Burma, and he seemed to be growing in influence. The Australian anthropologist Paul Cohen had traced the path of Khruba Bunchum also, finally meeting him in person at a festival for a renovated Buddhist stupa in Muang Sing, Laos.[11] The festival Cohen observed included the ritual offering of donations and candles to the reliquary by pilgrims, including up to two thousand Tai Lües from Sipsongpanna.[12]

In Muang Sing Khruba Bunchum was building another of his many reliquaries, all of which are situated in Tai border regions of the Mekong Delta. In 1998 Khruba Bunchum and his followers had built a reliquary on the Burmese side of the border a few miles from Da Menglong, the one Aye Zai Guang and his friends visited while I waited at the border. Khruba Bunchum invited a well-known elder changkhap from Sipsongpanna to sing at the opening ceremony. Burma's government was building Buddhas to mark the national borders, invoking a tradition of sacred kingship. But with his network of reliquaries, Khruba Bunchum and his followers were writing their own new map that crossed the borders of Thailand, Burma, and Laos, reviving what they called "Yuan Buddhism" in the regions around the Mekong Delta. China would not allow Khruba Bunchum to build a reliquary within its borders, but his brief annual visit drew thousands of Tai Lües from across Sipsongpanna for a brief glimpse of the emerging pan-Tai religious revival.

The construction of new reliquaries by Khruba Bunchum, the new printing projects, and the Tai Lüe pop music, along with old changkhap, were all "real Tai culture" according to Tai Lües in Sipsongpanna. Equally new temples built by the Chinese state were "fake." As one Tai Lüe villager put it, "There are fake temples and real temples. Real temples are the ones our Tai community uses. Fake temples are the ones the tourists go to." Real Tai identity had nothing to do with age or revival—it had to do with the presence and active participation of the Tai community.

Buddhas as Sites of Contest

> We say China is a country vast in territory, rich in resources and large in population; as a matter of fact, it is the Han nationality whose population is large and the minority nationalities whose territory is vast and whose resources are rich . . . .
>
> —MAO ZEDONG[13]

IN A REGION where ethnic religion has long been embedded in political struggles and in state power, it is perhaps unsurprising to see disagreements about the meaning of ethnic religious symbols.

The Buddha images described here—in theme parks, tourist towns, contested borderlands—are themselves arenas where state and non-state actors dispute each others' claims to material resources, religious authority, political power, even to the land itself. Because of the things the Buddha image represents—peace, sacrality, a hierarchical and transnational religious system—and because of the social history of this image in this region, the Buddha can be invoked to bolster a variety of positions and claims. In particular, the Burmese state, the Chinese state, and ethnic activists of various stripes have developed three tactical uses for the Buddha: they use him as a claim marker, as a semaphore to international observers, and as a consecrator of a safe space that is linked to other safe spaces across a network of similar Buddhas.

Buddhas That Stake Claims

BY BUILDING BUDDHA statues, temples, and reliquaries in ethnic regions of China and Burma, a variety of actors have staked claims to geographic terrain.

Khruba Bunchum's transnational Yuan Buddhist reliquary-building project is one example of this: it marks out a claim to a socially constructed tradition; a resistant, trans-border, pan-Tai geography. In truth, the geography that existed before the encroachment of China, Thailand, Laos, and Burma onto the Tai region was not unified but splintered among sometimes allied, sometimes warring city-states. Today, Khruba Bunchum and his followers build reliquaries that mark the Yuan Buddhist geography as a unified space outside of national borders. They have not said that their buddhas stake claims to the natural resources included in these religious borders, but a minority of Tais already talk of this religious geography as a political entity. It is possible that one day, if the region drastically destabilized, some activists might try to make political claims on this religious geography.

But similarly and on a larger scale, both China and Burma appear to be building Buddha images along the borders in ways that stake claims to the national borders and the resources in them. As Ma Yin helpfully observed, the three most important facts about

Chinese ethnic minorities—the three facts that make good management of their cultures by the state an urgent matter—are that these ethnic groups occupied the majority of China's arable land, that this land was rich in natural resources, and that it was strategically important to the defense of the new nation.

Buddhas as Signals to Investors

IN ORDER TO control these lands and resources, though, both China and Burma require infrastructure: roads, airports, and bridges that provide safe and rapid access to rivers, mines, and forests. The Asia Highway and roads like it, many of them funded or sanctioned by international financial institutions and individual foreign investors, were in principle built to facilitate trans-border trade. In practice, they not only provide access to transnational shipping routes, but also allow Burmese troops access to ethnic regions, and allow Chinese and Burmese officials and entrepreneurs quicker access to lumber and minerals in ethnic border regions. As international investors have helped to build major highways in China, China has in turn helped to build many of Burma's new roads and bridges and has trained and armed the Burmese junta's troops as they move down the new roads obliterating ethnic resistance. This in turn has brought a new kind of stability to the region, which also facilitates the plundering of forests and mines in northern Burma.

Because infrastructure projects are seen as benevolent forms of development, especially when linked to tourism, roads and bridges are magnets for international investors. Thus tourism development, including the development of religious sites as tourist destinations, has helped in some small way to consecrate two authoritarian states' almost total domination and reconfiguration of their shared border region. The buddhas built by China and Burma as tourist attractions—the Tai-style temples in theme parks, the Golden Buddha in Shan State—are like canaries in a gold mine, signaling to potential Chinese and international investors that the authoritarian states now have their troubled borders under control and that the borderlands are safe for investment.

Buddhas as Hubs on a Network

IRONICALLY, THOUGH, THIS final expansion of two authoritarian states to the limits of their own borders was only feasible after both closed states began to open their national borders to international investment and trade. Since the early 1990s, China, Burma, Laos, Thailand, and international banks have collaborated to "reduce bureaucratic and procedural constraints to cross-border trade," opening borders to "the free flow of goods and people."[14] The same forces that have powered China and Burma's conquest of their own borders is undermining the integrity of those borders. The rapid economic flows up and down the Mekong Delta can uproot villages and rice fields, relocate whole populations, lay mountains bare, and reshape the landscape. They displace ethnic minorities intended as the beneficiaries of trans-border development and bring these disaffected peoples together in bus stations, flophouses, construction sites, markets, and—of course—Buddhist temples.

Ethnic inequalities around the Mekong Delta—minorities' lack of education, capital, and opportunities to participate in the development gold rush on an equal basis with majority peoples—fuel the passions with which Tais connect, through their temples, with one another across the borders. Some of these new and old temples in Sipsongpanna, Shan State, and elsewhere in the region have become hubs on a network of like-minded Buddhists. The Buddhist temple system is becoming a conduit through which Tais in one region access the capital, technology, and information of Tais in another region.

This emergence of religious trans-border networks is obviously not unique to the Mekong Delta. Arjun Appadurai elsewhere calls these "diasporic public spheres" and "ethnoscapes" and considers them one mark of globalization.[15] But while Appadurai notes the electronic face of these ethnoscapes—the ways they use new media to create a globalizing ethnic community—he may not adequately credit the value of the small group in building a trans-border network. In an age of high-speed Internet and mass television broadcasts, the Tai revival is growing mostly through small, face-to-face gatherings of travelers who meet in multiple, similar, sacred halls located up and down the Mekong. Here they give an offering to the Buddha, hear a sermon or a narration, share a prayer, and exchange cassettes, computer disks, and DVDs by hand.

Conclusions

IN JULY 2002, with grants from the Ford Foundation and from UCLA, I coordinated a small conference in Chiang Mai, Thailand, to further explore cultural change and cultural survival in Sipsongpanna. A group of Sipsongpanna Tai Lüe journalists, officials, and lay temple activists came to meet with Thai and American scholars, archivists, and foundation consultants. We chose Chiang Mai as the site for reasons of logistics and cost, but what ensued was in retrospect probably foreseeable: the serious scholarly conference virtually turned into a three-day festival in celebration of the pan-Tai revival. Our colleagues at Chiang Mai University put together a tour for the "cousins from Sipsongpanna," who rode in state in a hired van from school to museum to temple, greeted everywhere by crowds of northern Thai elders, children, singers, dancers, and monks. E Guang, one of the featured panelists, sang changkhap songs at each stop for admiring Thai audiences. Aye Zai Guang walked in amazement through a small local museum housing northern Thai relics that reminded him of things he had not seen since childhood in Sipsongpanna. The lively panel presentations—translated noisily and simultaneously into Chinese, Thai, Tai Lüe, other Tai languages, and English—were interspersed with lengthy social meals and toasts of rice liquor and Thai whiskey that lasted late into each night.

As one of these meals gradually wound down one evening, I sat at a table catching up on the past few years with E La and Aye Nawn. Aye Nawn had succeeded in producing a series of Tai Lüe karaoke DVDs, just as he had dreamed of doing a few years earlier, and had ambitious plans for many more. E La had become a traveling entrepreneur, running a small restaurant in one town, translating for a Chinese business delegation to Thailand in another, traveling up and down the Mekong in pursuit of her next, big, business opportunity.

As we spoke about the conference, I asked them the intractable question about Sipsongpanna: Why is it that while the Chinese government cracks down so brutally on Uyghur and Tibetan ethnic activists it is relatively tolerant of Tai Lües?

E La answered first: "The Chinese government obliterated our culture during the Cultural Revolution. There was nothing left. As far as they know, we don't have any culture left, and so they trust us."

Aye Nawn nodded and added, "What's more, we are not *hao dou*,"—a Chinese word used for someone who enjoys a fight. "Those other nationalities are combative, and we are not. The government has no reason to oppress us."

Aye Nawn and E La were suggesting that in Sipsongpanna the state ignores the ethnic cultural and religious revival that it would be inconvenient to see, and ethnic activists avoid forcing the state to see these things. However, China has established its hold on the national borders in many ways through the careful management of ethnic culture and identity. As the Tai Lüe movement grows and its trans-border links strengthen, can the Chinese state continue to politely ignore, as it were, the elephant sitting in its living room? The answer may be yes, as long as the Tai revival is willing and able to carefully, quietly negotiate its demands behind the scenes.

This book has argued that for over fifty years, the People's Republic of China has worked to build a whole nation out of what had been a collapsed empire. To do so it has legitimized its rule over the ethnic borderlands by creating a new national civilization, a new Chinese culture. Beijing was the high center of this new national identity, an advanced socialist civilization unified by a new vernacular language and simplified script. Peripheral peoples such as the Tai Lüe were described as uncivilized and in need of Beijing's leadership in order to become "advanced."

As part of this process of national reinvention, the Chinese government created new texts and songs for and about ethnic minorities, cultural forms that simplified and often misrepresented ethnic minority cultures. The state drew heavily on ethnic folklore but altered this to conform to long-standing imperial stereotypes about ethnic primitivity and naïveté, and to new ideals of national identity. Elements of earlier ethnic cultural practices and indigenous institutions that did not fit into the new state-constructed ethnic identities were actively erased and suppressed. What is referred to here as the "simplifying project" was part of a state-centric process in which the borders were brought under control, ethnic land was claimed for the center, and material resources were appropriated for the developing nation. Gradually, the state created the ethnic groups it needed to justify its rule of the valuable borderlands—a low border against which the ruling center seemed high.

In order to be high, the national culture needs to be surrounded by things that are lower. If its internal Others are not low enough to justify the civilizing rhetoric of the center, then the domination of smaller kingdoms by larger ones and the exploitation of their material resources becomes less obviously benevolent. Every Harvard must have its wild Indians. If the peripheral peoples are seen to have "caught up with" or are arguably cultural peers of the high civilization the whole hierarchy risks collapsing into a congeries of feuding equal centers.

As the new nation emerged, ethnic border peoples learned to present themselves in ways that Chinese officials would find appealing and acceptable. More recently, this had been reinforced and capitalized through the economic development of tourism, which created ethnic theme parks, dance halls, and hotels, patronized mostly by Chinese tourists. Thus tourism had also helped to incorporate Yunnan more fully into the Chinese nation—the road to China's borders has been paved by ethnic dancing women. Today, with substantial assistance from China, it appears that Burma is well on its way toward emulating the Chinese model.

But cultural production has become the sphere in which contests between the state and locals over political autonomy and material resources are quietly fought. Off the front stage, in interstitial spaces emerging in temples and villages, Tai Lüe minorities are reviving historical relationships with other Tais across the borders and are reviving and reinventing Tai Lüe oral, textual, and Buddhist culture. Growing numbers of Tais, though not all, talk about their local revivals in terms of a trans-border, shared sphere, though they continue to debate about where this revival is heading.

As yet, this pan-Tai revival is fractured, localized, and decentralized. It is certainly not a nationalist movement imagining a single capital of a future, unified nation-state. The absence of genuine pan-Tai nationalism (if one accepts that this is in fact an absence, a lack) may owe to the history of the region, which long had multiple small centers and never had a single capital or one shared script. Today, the upper Mekong Delta has multiple vectors of nostalgia and loyalty. While some Jinghong activists may speak nostalgically of Kengtung or Chiang Mai, other activists in Chiang Mai speak nostalgically of Sipsongpanna, and so on. Thus the emerging network does not much resemble incipient nationalism as described by Anderson and others. Rather, the network functions with roughly co-equal hubs that exchange capital, information, monks, technology, and goods.

As Aye Nawn pointed out, given the existing balance of powers, there is no reason for an open confrontation between the Chinese state and the Tai Lüe revival. And despite the looming example of the former Soviet Union, and China's related fears about Taiwanese and Tibetan independence, as Appadurai observes in another context, not all ethnic revivals lead inevitably to separatism: "In most cases of . . . ethnic revival on a large scale, the common thread is self-determination rather than territorial sovereignty as such."[16] Given the elastic space allotted to the Tai Lües in China, their revival will probably remain peaceable unless they begin to demand greater autonomy than the state is willing to grant them.

Should this happen and should the Chinese state begin to jail, torture, and execute Tai activists as it has their counterparts in Xinjiang and Tibet, then Yunnan's Tai Lües could be propelled into confrontation. A brutal crackdown by China on Yunnan's borders would radicalize many minorities, especially those that have already been cut adrift by the region's economic destabilization. Such a crackdown could throw Chinese ethnic activists into the arms of related ethnic rebels in Burma and launch them together into an open and armed resistance against both states.

Many other Tai Lües, though, would probably not take up arms. Instead, they would do what family members did a generation ago: bury the old texts and Buddha images under the stilt house, gather any monks, singers, or activists in the family, pack a bag, and start walking: through the rice fields, through the forests, over the mountains, across the borders, to find a quiet village in which to wait.

Notes

Introduction. The Writing on the Wall

1. In 1990, Burma's military junta, the State Law and Order Restoration Council, refused to recognize the results of a democratic election that would have awarded power to the opposition party led by Daw Aung San Suu Kyi. Instead, SLORC changed its name to the State Peace and Development Council and changed the country's name to Myanmar, as if to signal a new beginning. Many international scholars and activists continue to refer to the country as Burma.

2. This name may in turn derive from Varanasi (Benares), according to legend the birthplace of the Buddha.

3. Hsieh Shi-chung, "On the Dynamics of Tai/Dai-Lüe Ethnicity: An Ethnohistorical Analysis," in *Cultural Encounters on China's Ethnic Frontiers*, ed. Stevan Harrell (Seattle: University of Washington Press, 1995), 301–28.

4. Some Chinese anthropology texts confusingly refer to such groupings as "Shui Dai" ("Water Tai"), "Huayao Dai" ("Flower-Belt Tai"), "Han Dai" ("Han Chinese Dai"), and so on; specifics of lifestyle and costume are attributed to each. Tai Lüe scholars interviewed in Sipsongpanna assert that, unlike the term "Tai Lüe," these are not indigenous ethnic names.

5. The following discussion is indebted to Pierre Bourdieu, *The Field of Cultural Production* (New York: Columbia University Press, 1993). In it, Bourdieu describes the literary or artistic field of a given period and society as a "field of struggles" between individuals occupying various literary or artistic positions. Occupants of these

different positions take various strategies in order to defend their positions or to increase their power relative to others in the same field. One common strategy is to make claims of authenticity or to assert one's ability to judge, for instance, what is or is not "really" art, but in fact, says Bourdieu, "If there is a truth, it is that truth is a stake in the struggle" (262).

6. Ma Yin, *China's Minority Nationalities* (Beijing: Foreign Languages Press, 1989), 3.

7. In June 2001, Tai Lües in Shan State, Burma, who were originally from Sipsongpanna, told me they had fought in insurgencies against China that were supported by the U.S. CIA during the 1950s. See also Bertil Lintner, "The CIA's First Secret War: Americans Helped Stage Raids Into China from Burma," *Far Eastern Economic Review*, 16 September 1993, 56–58.

8. Benedict Anderson, *Imagined Communities: Reflections on the Origin and Spread of Nationalism* (London: Verso Press, 1983), 13.

9. Ibid.

10. Victor H. Mair, *Anthologizing and Anthropologizing: The Place of Non-elite and Non-standard Culture in the Chinese Literary Tradition*, Working Papers in Asian/Pacific Studies (Durham, N.C.: Asian/Pacific Studies Institute, Duke University, 1992), 24; later edited and republished in *Translating Chinese Literature*, ed. Eugene Eoyang and Lin Yaofu (Bloomington: Indiana University Press, 1995).

11. Stevan Harrell, "Introduction: Civilizing Projects and the Reaction to Them," in *Cultural Encounters on China's Ethnic Frontiers*, ed. Stevan Harrell (Seattle: University of Washington Press, 1995), 4.

12. Ibid., 3.

13. Lu Xun, *Diary of a Madman and Other Stories*, trans. William A. Lyell (Honolulu: University of Hawai'i Press, 1990).

14. Y. C. Wang, *Chinese Intellectuals and the West, 1872–1949* (Chapel Hill: University of North Carolina Press, 1966), 308.

15. Wang, *Chinese Intellectuals*, 397.

16. Mao Zedong, *Talks at the Yenan Forum on Literature and Art*, 4th ed. (Beijing: Foreign Languages Press, 1967), 19.

17. Ibid.

18. Spoken Mandarin Chinese can vary dramatically from one region to another. Even the versions of spoken Mandarin used in two neighboring towns can sometimes be significant. While most English-speakers refer to Cantonese and other spoken variants of

Mandarin as "dialects," in fact some linguists argue that the differences in regional tongues are so significant that we should consider them to be different languages (Victor H. Mair, "What is a Chinese 'Dialect/Topolect'? Reflections on Some Key Sino-English Linguistic Terms," *Sino-Platonic Papers* 29 [September 1991]). Certainly not all visitors from other areas of China can understand *Yunnan hua* (Yunnanese), the spoken version of Chinese used by many residents of Yunnan. And many native speakers of Mandarin find *Jingjong hua* (Jinghong-ese), the Sipsongpanna variant of Yunnanese, to be largely incomprehensible.

19. Fei Xiaotong, *Toward a People's Anthropology* (Beijing: World Press, 1981), 60.

20. Fei, *People's Anthropology*, 64.

21. For Sipsongpanna, see for instance the "Minzu wenti wu zhong congshu," in *Xishuangbanna Daizu zhonghe diaocha* (Collected investigations into Xishuangbanna Dai nationality) (Kunming: Yunnan minzu chuban she, 1983).

22. Guojia minwei minzu wenti wu zhong congshu pianli weiyuanhui, ed., *Zhongguo shaoshu minzu* (Chinese ethnic minorities) (Beijing: Renmin chuban she, 1981), 342–43.

23. Ma Yin, *China's Minority Nationalities*, 266.

24. Sifabu faxue jiaocai bianjibu, ed., *Zhongguo minzu faxue* (Chinese nationalities law studies) (Beijing: Falu chuban she, 1996), 398.

25. Ibid., 402–4.

26. Yan Jiaqi and Gao Gao, *Turbulent Decade: A History of the Chinese Cultural Revolution*, trans. and ed. D. W. Y. Kwok (Honolulu: University of Hawai'i Press, 1996), 73–74.

27. Erik Mueggler, "Spectral Subversions: Rival Tactics of Time and Agency in Southwest China," *Comparative Studies in Society and History* 41, no. 3 (July 1999): 458–81.

28. See, for instance, "Trials of a Tibetan Monk: The Case of Tenzin Delek" (New York: Human Rights Watch, February 2004), available at http://hrw.org/reports/2004/china0204; and "Gross Violations of Human Rights in the Xinjiang Uighur Autonomous Region" (London: Amnesty International, April 1999), available at http://web.amnesty.org/library/Index/engASA170181999.

29. Mette Halskov Hansen, "The Call of Mao or Money? Han Chinese Settlers on China's South-Western Borders," *China Quarterly* 158 (June 1999): 397.

1. Front Stage

1. William Clifton Dodd, *The Tai Race, Elder Brother of the Chinese: Results of Experience, Exploration, and Research of William Clifton Dodd, D.D., Thirty-Three Years a Missionary to the Tai People of Siam, Burma, and China, Compiled and Edited by His Wife* (1923; Bangkok: White Lotus Press, 1996), 183.

2. Chris Taylor et al., *China: A Lonely Planet Travel Survival Kit* (Hawthorn, Australia: Lonely Planet, 1996), 770.

3. Thongchai Winichakul, *Siam Mapped: A History of the Geo-body of a Nation* (Chiang Mai, Thailand: Silkworm Books, 1994), shows how colonial mapping shaped the Sino-Lao-Thai borders.

4. Judith Shapiro, *Mao's War Against Nature: Politics and the Environment in Revolutionary China* (Cambridge: Cambridge University Press, 2001).

5. E. C. Chapman, "Plans and Realities in the Development of Trans-Mekong Transport Corridors: Reflections from Recent Fieldwork in the Upper Mekong Corridor," *Thai-Yunnan Project Newsletter* 29 (June 1995): 10–17. The "Asian values" were putatively shared not only by the four countries and their Japanese and Korean investors but also by the diverse ethnic minorities in each nation.

6. Dean MacCannell, *The Tourist: A New Theory of the Leisure Class* (Berkeley and Los Angeles: University of California Press, 1999).

7. For more on Splendid China, see Ann Anagnost, *National Past-times: Narrative, Representation, and Power in Modern China* (Durham, N.C.: Duke University Press, 1997).

8. Benedict Anderson, *Imagined Communities: Reflections on the Origin and Spread of Nationalism* (London: Verso Press, 1983), 9–12.

9. Anagnost, *National Past-times*, 163.

10. Kimberly J. Lau, "Serial Logic: Folklore and Difference in the Age of Feel-Good Multiculturalism," *Journal of American Folklore* 113 (1999): 70–82.

11. "Locked Doors: The Human Rights of People Living with HIV/AIDS in China" (New York: Human Rights Watch, 2003); available at http://www.hrw.org.

12. Jane Desmond, *Staging Tourism: Bodies on Display from Waikiki to Sea World* (Chicago: University of Chicago Press, 1999).

13. Jill Dolan, *The Feminist Spectator as Critic* (Ann Arbor, Mich.: UMI Research Press, 1988).

14. Barbara Kirshenblatt-Gimblett, *Destination Culture: Tourism, Museums, and Heritage* (Berkeley: University of California Press, 1998), 45.

15. Dru Gladney, "Representing Nationality in China: Refiguring Majority/ Minority Identities," *Journal of Asian Studies* 53 (February 1994): 92–123; and Louisa Schein, *Minority Rules: The Miao and the Feminine in China's Cultural Politics* (Durham, N.C.: Duke University Press, 2000).

16. All but a couple of the Manting Road cafés were closed in 1998 and 1999 during a campaign to crack down on sex tourism. However, other cafés with identical dance revues have since emerged in other locations around Jinghong, including one at the Xishuangbanna Binguan that is managed by the prefectural government.

17. Xishuangbanna Daizu zizhizhou minzu gewutuan fuwubu (Xishuangbanna Dai nationality autonomous prefecture song-and-dance troupe service department), ed., *Xishuangbanna fengqing: San duo jiao* (Xishuangbanna atmosphere: Three stamps of the foot), performed by Xishuangbanna Song-and-Dance Troupe, Zhongguo changpian zong gongsi Chengdu gongsi chuban faxing (China central recording company, Chengdu company production) JH-29, 1992, audiocassette.

18. Hui Yingzhao, lyrics; Shen Qiwu, melody; Dong Bingchang, accompaniment; "Xishuangbanna, wode jiaxiang" (Xishuangbanna, my hometown), *Xishuangbanna fengqing: San duo jiao* (Xishuangbanna atmosphere: Three stamps of the foot), performed by Xishuangbanna Song-and-Dance Troupe, Zhongguo changpian zong gongsi Chengdu gongsi chuban faxing (China central recording company, Chengdu company production) JH-29, 1992, audiocassette.

19. Edward Schafer, *The Vermillion Bird: T'ang Images of the South* (Berkeley: University of California Press, 1967), 82.

20. Ibid., 84–85.

21. Norma Diamond, "The Miao and Poison: Interactions on China's Southwest Frontier," *Ethnology* 27, no. 1 (January 1988): 1–25.

22. Charles F. McKhann, "The Naxi and the Nationalities Question," in *Cultural Encounters on China's Ethnic Frontiers*, ed. Stevan Harrell (Seattle: University of Washington Press, 1995), 35.

23. See, for example, David K. Wyatt and Aroonrut Wichienkeeo, trans., *The Chiang Mai Chronicle*, 2nd ed. (Chiang Mai, Thailand: Silkworm Books, 1998); and Xishuangbanna Daizu zizhizhou wenhua ju (Xishuangbanna Dai nationality autonomous region culture bureau), ed., *Zanha ju zhi* (A record of changkhap opera) (Beijing: Wenhua yishu chuban she, 1993), 140.

24. For instance, compare the excerpted translation of the Tai Lüe "Sithat auk boht" in chapter 4 with Donald K. Swearer's translation of the northern Thai monastic text "Sittha ok buat," which he translates as

"Siddhattha's Renunciation," in *Becoming the Buddha: The Ritual of Image Consecration in Thailand* (Princeton, N.J.: Princeton University Press, 2004), 138–51. Swearer has studied other monastic texts from northern Thailand and also describes a version of "Ga peuk" (The white crow) very similar to descriptions of the song heard in Sipsongpanna. Finally, Peltier's translation of the Lanna text of the "Pathamamulamuli" (Origin of the world) from Chiang Mai resembles the version of the "Pathamala" that is still recounted orally in Sipsongpanna, according to descriptions of it given by Tai Lüe changkhap poets (Anatole-Roger Peltier, *Pathamamulamuli: L'Origine du monde selon la tradition du Lan Na; The Origin of the World in the Lan Na Tradition*, published in Chiang Mai, photocopy). Tai Lüe poets described the "Pathamala" as the most advanced and challenging text for a changkhap to learn and said that women poets were not taught it. References to a poem by the same name in Sipsongpanna can be found in a fascinating medieval text, written by a Tai Lüe Buddhist bishop and available in Chinese translation: Chuba Meng (in Tai, "Khuba Muang"), *Lun Daizu shige* (A discussion of Tai poetry and song) (in Tai, "Wa du ma yaw gamkhap Tai"), trans. Ai Wenpian (Kunming: Zhongguo minjian wenxue chuban she, 1981). However, note that some of Ai Wenpian's translations may have been altered to reflect contemporary Chinese policies, so they cannot be considered authoritative. The Tai Lüe original version of "Pathamala" has not been published. For more on *molam* (a genre related to changkhap) in Laos, see Carol Compton, *Courting Poetry in Laos: A Textual and Linguistic Analysis* (DeKalb: Northern Illinois University Center for Southeast Asian Studies, 1979).

25. In 2004, Dubi Long Zhaum, the abbot of Wat Pajay, was promoted to the status of *khuba* (in Thai, "*khruba*"), changing his name to "Khuba Zhaum."

2. Song and Silence

1. "Dao" is the title of Tai Lüe members of the noble class and "Zhao" is the title of the prince's family.
2. Guan Jian, *The Indigenous Religion and Theravada Buddhism in Ban Da Tiu, a Dai Lue Village in Yunnan (China)*, vol. 2 of *Tai Minorities in China* (Gaya, India: Centre for Southeast Asian Studies, 1993).
3. E (often "Yu" in Chinese) is the surname for all Tai Lüe women in Sipsongpanna.

4. Hasegawa Kiyoshi, "Cultural Revival and Ethnicity: The Case of the Tai Lue in the Sipsong Panna, Yunnan Province" (24 January 2001); available at http://coe.asafas.kyoto-u.ac.jp/research/sea/social/hayashi.

5. Xishuangbanna Daizu zizhizhou wenhua ju (Xishuangbanna Dai nationality autonomous region culture bureau), ed., *Zanha juzhi* (A record of changkhap opera) (Beijing: Wenhua yishu chuban she, 1993). In 1998 and 1999 a group of Sipsongpanna culture-bureau officials started up the changkhap opera troupe again; it gave several performances before encountering financial difficulties.

6. Ma Hsueh-liang, "Minority Languages of China," *China Reconstructs* (May/June 1954): 40–41.

7. William Clifton Dodd, *The Tai Race,Elder Brother of the Chinese: Results of Experience, Exploration, and Research of William Clifton Dodd, D.D., Thirty-Three Years a Missionary to the Tai People of Siam, Burma, and China, Compiled and Edited by His Wife* (1923; Bangkok: White Lotus Press, 1996), 188.

8. Ibid., 187.

9. Evelyn Rawski, "Economic and Social Foundations of Late Imperial China," in *Popular Culture in Late Imperial China*, ed. David Johnson, Andrew Nathan, and Evelyn Rawski (Berkeley: University of California Press, 1985), 11.

10. See also interviews with administrators at Sipsongpanna schools and colleges in which they explicitly state that their aim is to facilitate the phasing out of Tai language; Mette Halskov Hansen, *Lessons in Being Chinese: Minority Education and Ethnic Identity in Southwest China* (Seattle: University of Washington Press, 1999), 129–30.

11. All Tai Lüe men in Sipsongpanna who are not members of the nobility are surnamed "Aye" ("Ai" in Mandarin). Those who initiate as novices are given a new surname, "Pha," which means novice. If the novice ordains as a monk his surname changes to "Du;" if he becomes a senior monk it becomes "Dubi." "Dubi Long" means "Great Senior Monk" and is the title for an abbot. An ordained monk who returns to lay life is given a new surname, "Khanan," as a recognition of his advanced education.

12. The use of the term "Tai Khun" here is interesting. Tais in Sipsongpanna are Tai Lüe, and the term Tai Khun is used mostly for Tais who live around the city of Kengtung in Shan State. Tai Khun script is very similar to Tai Lüe script, as is the spoken language, and the regions are closely connected in many ways. Early Tai Lüe pop imitated Tai

Khun pop and rock, and that may be why the songwriter chose to call Sipsongpanna residents Tai Khun here.

13. "Sao Tai bai fon Muang Haw" (The Tai girl goes to dance in the Han region), *Aye Sam khaphawng* (Aye Sam sings), performed by Aye Sam and the New Star Band, Yunnan yinxiang chuban she chuban (Yunnan sound and images production company production) H-522, 1997, audiocassette.

14. Muang Long is the Tai Lüe name for the town known as Da Menglong in Chinese.

15. The monk, called Dubi Gang here, has since left monastic life and now lives abroad, where he still writes and records songs.

16. Craig A. Lockhard, *Dance of Life: Popular Music and Politics in Southeast Asia* (Honolulu: University of Hawai'i Press, 1998), xii.

17. Ibid., 185.

18. Ibid.

19. I was in Kunming renewing my research visa when the first concert took place and so was not able to attend.

20. Rice or salt wrapped in banana leaves are traditional love tokens.

21. Perry Link, *The Uses of Literature: Life in the Socialist Chinese Literary System* (Princeton, N.J.: Princeton University Press, 2000), 91.

22. Joan N. Radner and Susan S. Lanser, "Strategies of Coding in Women's Cultures," in *Feminist Messages: Coding in Women's Folk Culture,* ed. Joan N. Radner (Urbana: University of Illinois Press, 1993), 1–30.

23. James C. Scott, *Domination and the Arts of Resistance: Hidden Transcripts* (New Haven, Conn.: Yale University Press, 1990).

3. The Oral Poet Laureate

1. Kanglang Zhai (Khanan Zhuai), *Dai jiaren zhi ge* (Songs of the Dai family) (Kunming: Yunnan renmin chuban she, 1979).

2. Margaret Mills, *Rhetorics and Politics in Afghan Traditional Storytelling* (Philadelphia: University of Pennsylvania Press, 1990), 14.

3. See, for example, Richard Bauman, *Verbal Art as Performance* (Prospect Heights, Ill.: Waveland Press, 1977); and Daniel Ben-Amos and Kenneth S. Goldstein, eds., *Folklore: Performance and Communication* (The Hague: Mouton, 1975).

4. Charles L. Briggs, *Competence in Performance: The Creativity of Tradition in Mexicano Verbal Art* (Philadelphia: University of Pennsylvania Press, 1988), 372.

5. Historically, the *muang*, or small city-states, that made up Sipsong-panna were aligned as a federation of equals. Each *muang* was ruled by a nobleman who was in turn, ruled over by a *chao phaendin*, literally "ruler of the land." Because the prince was generally viewed as first among equals and could be deposed and replaced by the nobility if he did not perform to their satisfaction, the term *chao phaendin* is generally translated in English as "prince." For more on premodern Tai Lüe political structures, see Sara Davis, "Premodern Flows in Postmodern China: Globalization and the Sipsongpanna Tais," *Modern China* 29.2 (April 2003): 176–203.

6. Quan Quan, "Lun zanhade chansheng he fazhan" (Discussion of the emergence and development of changkhap), in *Beiye wenhua lun* (Discussion of palm-leaf manuscript culture), ed. Wang Yizhi and Chang Shiguang (Kunming: Yunnan renmin chuban she, 1990), 495–502.

7. Because women could not ordain as monks and study in Buddhist temples they therefore lacked the education that would prepare them to perform Buddhist epics competitively.

8. Zhang Cuifeng, "My Life as a Drumsinger: The Autobiography of Jang Tsueyfenq [Zhang Cuifeng]," trans. Rulan Chao Pian, *Chinese Oral and Performing Literature (CHINOPERL) Papers* 13 (1984/1985): 32–33.

9. Bauman, *Verbal Art*, 11.

10. See Milman Parry and Albert Bates Lord, eds., *Serbocroatian Heroic Songs; Volume One: Novi Pazar: English Translations* (Cambridge and Belgrade: Harvard University Press and the Serbian Academy of Sciences, 1954); Albert Bates Lord, *The Singer of Tales* (Cambridge: Harvard University Press, 1960); and Dennis Tedlock, *The Spoken Word and the Work of Interpretation* (Philadelphia: University of Pennsylvania Press, 1983).

11. Tedlock, *Spoken Word*, 55; and Jerome Rothenberg, *Shaking the Pumpkin: Traditional Poetry of the Indian North Americas* (Garden City, N.Y.: Doubleday, 1972), xxii–xxiii.

12. Chen Hanseng, "Thai People of Yunnan," *China Reconstructs* (September/October 1953): 38.

13. Ibid.

14. Patrick Hanan, a scholar of Chinese vernacular literature, notes the same technique in China's earliest novels, which worked in faux-oral language and stylistic tricks to enliven written narratives by making them sound as if they were recounted by oral storytellers. Patrick Hanan, *The Chinese Vernacular Story*, Harvard East Asian

Series 94 (Cambridge: Harvard University Council on East Asian Studies, 1981).

15. *The Seven Sisters: Collected Chinese Folk Stories* (Beijing: Foreign Languages Press, 1965).

16. Hung Chang-tai, *Going to the People: Chinese Intellectuals and Folk Literature, 1918–1937* (Cambridge: Harvard University Press, 1985), 1.

17. Ibid., 1–2.

18. *Daizu jianshi bianxie zu* (Simple history of the Dai nationality editorial group), *Daizu jianshi* (Simple history of the Dai nationality) (Kunming: Yunnan renmin chuban she, 1986).

19. Yan Wenbian, Zheng Peng, and Gu Qing, eds. and adapters, *Dai Folk Legends* (Beijing: Foreign Languages Press, 1988), ii.

20. Benedict Anderson, *Imagined Communities: Reflections on the Origin and Spread of Nationalism* (London: Verso Press, 1983), 36.

21. Lucien Miller, ed., *South of the Clouds: Tales from Yunnan*, trans. Guo Xu, Lucien Miller, and Xu Kun (Seattle: University of Washington Press, 1994), 27.

22. Ibid., 36.

23. Chin Ming, "How the Peacock Dance Reached the Stage," *China Reconstructs* (March 1963): 10. I am indebted to Helen Rees for sharing this article with me.

24. Ibid., 11.

25. Kanglang Zhai [Khanan Zhuai], *Dai jiaren zhi ge*.

4. The Monks

1. Donald Swearer, "Hypostasizing the Buddha: Buddha Image Consecration in Northern Thailand," *History of Religions* 34 (February 1995): 279.

2. Further details, including original song texts in Tai Lüe and English, may be found in Sara L. M. Davis, "Singers of Sipsongbanna: Folklore and Authenticity in Contemporary China" (Ph.D. diss., University of Pennsylvania, 1999).

Conclusion. Buddhas on the Borders

1. Frank S. Jannuzi, "The New Burma Road (Paved by Polytechnologies?)," in *Burma: Prospects for a Democractic Future*, ed. Robert I. Rothberg (Washington, D.C.: World Peace Foundation, 1998), 197–208.

2. "Dispossessed: A Report of Forced Relocation and Extrajudicial Killings in Shan State, Burma" (Shan Human Rights Foundation, April 1998), available at www.shanland.org/HR/Publication/Dis/dispossessed.htm; "License to Rape: The Burmese Military Regime's Use of Sexual Violence in the Ongoing War in Shan State" (SHRF and Shan Women's Action Network, May 2002), available at www.shanland.org/HR/Publication/wa/contents.htm; and *Human Rights Yearbooks* (National Coalition Government of Burma, 1995–2003), available at www.ncgub.net/NCGUB/NCGUB%20Publications.htm.

3. Roger Moody, *Grave Diggers: A Report on Mining in Burma* (Vancouver: Canada Asia Pacific Resource Network, 1999); and *At What Price? Gold Mining in Kachin State, Burma* (Chiang Mai, Thailand: Images Asia / Ecology Desk, 2004).

4. Moody, *At What Price?*.

5. Like "Tai Lüe," the term "Tai Yai" refers to a population of Tai-speaking peoples in Shan State. Some people in Kengtung and the area around it call themselves "Tai Khun."

6. Aung Zaw, "Shwedagon and the Generals," *Irrawaddy News Magazine* 7, no. 4 (1999); available at http://www.irrawaddy.org/database/1999/vol7.4/coverstory.html.

7. See Jan Donkers and Minka Nijhuis, *Burma Behind the Mask* (Amsterdam: Burma Centrum Nederland, 1996). Tais pointed out a park constructed for tourists in Kengtung and said that the area surrounding it had been forcibly cleared of Tai Khun villages the year before. In their place was a sign lettered in English with rocks on the ground that read, strangely, "Have a nice life."

8. "Burma Tourism Boycott to Escalate Following Crackdown" (Burma Campaign UK, 11 June 2003); available at www.burmacampaign.org.uk/pm/more.php?id = 47_0_1_0_M.

9. Donald Swearer, *Buddhism and Society in Southeast Asia* (Chambersburg, Pa.: Anima Books, 1981), 138; and Thongchai Winichakul, *Siam Mapped: A History of the Geo-body of a Nation* (Chiang Mai, Thailand: Silkworm Books, 1994), 24.

10. Swearer, *Buddhism and Society*, 138.

11. Paul T. Cohen, "Lüe Across Borders: Pilgrimage and the Muang Sing Reliquary in Northern Laos," in *Where China Meets Southeast Asia: Social and Cultural Change in the Border Regions*, ed. Grant Evans, Chris Hutton, and Kuah Khun Eng (New York: St. Martin's Press, 2000), 145–61.

12. Ibid., 154.

13. Mao Zedong, *Selected Works of Mao Tse-tung*, vol. 5 (Beijing: Foreign Language Press, 1977), 295–96.

14. "Asian Highway Homepage," available at http://www.unescap.org/tctd/ah/introduct.htm, accessed 25 September 2001; and *Asian Highway* brochures, obtained from United Nations Economic and Social Commission for Asia and the Pacific, November 2001.

15. Arjun Appadurai, *Modernity at Large: Cultural Dimensions of Globalization* (Minneapolis: University of Minnesota Press, 1996), 21–41.

16. Ibid., 21.

Suggested Readings

MUCH OF THIS book is influenced by three books: Michael Hechter, *Internal Colonialism: The Celtic Fringe in British National Development, 1536–1966* (London: Routledge, 1975), on how economic domination shapes ethnicity; Thongchai Winichakul, *Siam Mapped: A History of the Geo-body of a Nation* (Chiang Mai, Thailand: Silkworm Books, 1994), on mapping and the politics of the Mekong Delta; and James C. Scott, *Seeing Like a State: How Certain Schemes to Improve the Human Condition Have Failed* (New Haven, Conn.: Yale University Press, 1998), on almost everything else. Martin Mowforth and Ian Munt, *Tourism and Sustainability: Development and New Tourism in the Third World* (London: Routledge, 2003), is also recommended for its combination of Marxian outrage and sharp wit. And two books on methods—Peggy Golde, ed., *Women in the Field: Anthropological Experiences* (Berkeley: University of California Press, 1986), and Bruce Jackson's classic *Fieldwork* (Urbana: University of Illinois Press, 1987)—along with a steady diet of Dove Bars, helped me personally with the ups and downs of fieldwork.

On China

THERE ARE MANY good books in English about Yunnan, including: Mette Halskov Hansen, *Lessons in Being Chinese: Minority Education and Ethnic Identity in Southwest China* (Seattle: University of Washington Press, 1999); and Erik Mueggler, *The Age of Wild Ghosts:*

Memory, Violence, and Place in Southwest China (Berkeley and Los Angeles: University of California Press, 2001). Ai Feng, Wang Song, and Dao Baorong, *Daizu wenxue shi* (History of Dai nationality literature) (Kunming: Yunnan minzu chuban she, 1995), contains discussions of old Tai Lüe as well as Chinese historical texts on many subjects, including but not limited to literature. For an account of grassroots activism in China, see Ian Johnson, *Wild Grass: Three Stories of Change in Modern China* (New York: Pantheon, 2004). For information about abuses against Tibetans and Uyghurs in China, see reports on the Web sites of Human Rights Watch, www.hrw.org, and Amnesty International, www.amnesty.org.

On Burma

BERTIL LINTNER, *Land of Jade: A Journey from India Through Northern Burma to China* (Bangkok: White Lotus, 1996), is an adventure tale packed with information and insight. Inge Sargent, *Twilight Over Burma: My Life as a Shan Princess* (Honolulu: University of Hawai'i Press, 1994), offers a glimpse of Tai life before the junta.

Tai Lüe Songs

IT IS CHALLENGING to find the music discussed in this book outside of the region. In Jinghong, Yunnan, new Tai Lüe pop and changkhap recordings are sold in gift shops near Wat Pajay (in Chinese, "Zong Fosi"). Visitors to Thailand can cross the border at the town of Mae Sai to visit Tachilek, Burma, for a day or longer. "Music Tai" shops in Tachilek sell Sipsongpanna Tai Lüe pop recordings, as well as others by Burmese Tai rock stars such as Sai Mao.

Index